This book could not have been w
of everyone I have come in contact with one way or another.
are all over this book. Thank you.

Dedication

This book is dedicated to everyone seeking knowledge out there.

Disclaimer

All the information contained in this book is purely for educational activities only. The writer does not assert the accuracy or wholesomeness of any info gotten from this book. The views contained within the pages of this material are those of the author in its

entirety. The author/writer will not be held accountable or liable for any missing information, omissions or errors, damages, injuries, or any losses that may occur from the use of information gotten from this book.

Contents

Chapter One

You have had it in mind for some time now on how to go about crafting with leather, but you never made that all-important move until you picked up this book. This is the all-important step towards learning what leatherworking and the intricacies of this art are all about. The basic questions involved before getting started are;

What is leather?

What tools and supplies do you need to have available?

What type of projects can you get started with as a beginner?

The questions will come in fast and furious, and you haven't gotten a suitable answer to set you on the right path. You are in the right place as this book will guide you with everything you need to know about leather and leatherworking either as a newbie with no idea at all about the craft or as a seasoned hand that needs to refresh the well of knowledge.

What is leather?

Leather is as old as man himself, and the survival of man through the ages is based, to no small extent, the availability of this material. Leather provides warmth and comfort during the cold seasons, but they were also used as a means of communication far before the advent of paper. The skins of animals hunted also served as housing, which protected families against the worst elements.

Recent discoveries show that leather materials used by ancient man as far back as 3000 years ago were still in pristine conditions. The way the leather artifacts and materials were used passed on a sense of importance and ranking to the individual using it within a community. A study of the history of times past showed that only folks who had some form of wealth were able to buy materials constructed from leather such as boots, leather parchments for storing of information, etc.

The art of working on leather to produce exquisite materials was an exclusive preserve of a few individuals who were very secretive about the trade secrets which they only revealed to deserving members of their families. When the Spaniards discovered the New World, they came along with skilled leather guildsmen who made use of the patterns and new environment to motivate new projects on leatherworks. This new beginning was the leap from how leather was worked on into the modern age of leatherworking that we have today.

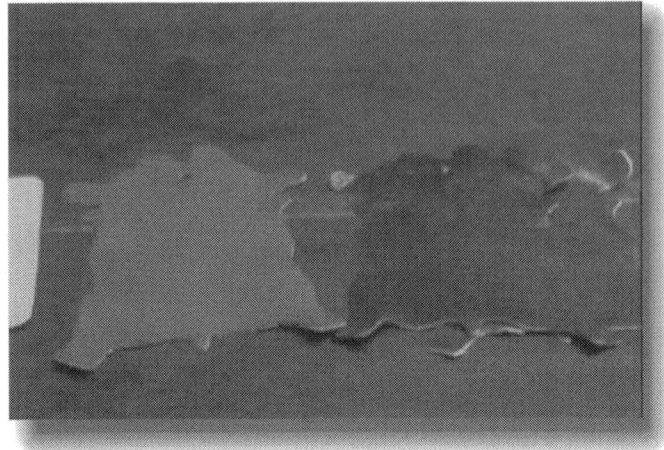

Nowadays, the art of or working with leather is one that any interested party can learn. The essential tools that anyone should have to work with leather successfully include and are not limited to the following; pear shader, veiner, beveller, swivel knife, mallet, backgrounder, seeder, etc. With experience and time spent working with leather, you will discover more specific tools to add to your toolbox and craft to churn out great masterpieces. Not forgetting the primary material without which the whole process cannot take place; leather.

Leather, on its own, stands out from any type of material or covering that man has ever worked on. Leather is the outer covering found on animals, mostly on oxen, cows, camels, horses, etc. These are the most common sources of leather used for this craft. For the skin to be easily worked on, it must undergo some form of processing, such as tanning.

In acquiring leather for your work, you can purchase it online and walk into that specialty store where the material is sold per square foot. When you flip the leather over to view the underside, you will most times notice markings that indicating the number of square feet. The signing is usually made with a machine stamp, chalk, or marker. The leather obtained from the animal is commonly referred to as the skin, and it may come to the market whole as it was taken from the animal or cut into various parts from the animal such as the shoulders, rump, belly, back, and sides.

Leather comes in varying thickness, and this is measured in ounces (1 ounce = 1/64 inch). This implies that four to five-ounce is 4/64 inch or 5/64 inch. The thickness of the leather is dependent on the source, with leather from cow and oxen been thicker than those gotten from a calf. The thickness also varies according to the part of the animal's body from which it was obtained. To have an evenly distributed depth in the whole leather or the different portions, the leather is processed in a splitting machine. This only aims to even out the thickness, which is a complicated process because of the leather's moisture content; it is run through the machine. The unevenness is why there is never an exact weight stamped on the leather; hence you will see weight measurements such as 5-6 oz, 8-9 oz, etc.

Now let us get into a detailed explanation of what leather is.

Leather is obtained from various animal skins, which, after undergoing a series of chemical and physical processes to prevent deterioration and improve its quality, will then be used for multiple items. When the skin of animals is viewed closely, throw a microscope, it will be observed that it is composed of numerous interconnecting fibers called collagen. On the outside, however, the skin is the largest organ on most animals that covers the internal organs. This outer part of the skin is termed the epidermis and acts as a barrier against the physical external and, most times, harmful surroundings.

Leather Uses

Leather has many desirable qualities that singles it out for a wide variety of uses, both domestic and outdoors. Some of such unique features of leather that makes it a favorite for artisans includes;

-       Hydrophobic nature, with this quality, leather can be used in the production of clothes, shoes, and other human apparel due to its ability to breathe and, at the same time, prevent the entry of moisture.

-       Resistance nature; the unique physical and chemical composition of leather makes it ideal for making use of in a lot of products that are in constant use; hence they do not undergo the wearing down that some other materials will experience. The leather resistance is different based on the source of the material, the finishing it has undergone, tanning, thickness, etc.

-       The pleasing aesthetics; this is a valuable and often looked out for feature of leather. The color, wrinkles, smell and general outlook of a piece of leather general makes it a more acceptable material for leatherworks or not.

-       The Feel; the easily identifiable and lovable touch that one gets from leather makes it a highly coveted material used for those priced materials. It is common to come across synthetic leather, which will have features that are not the same as natural leather. Such materials will most times look similar to natural leather, but they cannot synthesize that unique resistance and feel they get from the real deal.

-       The hygiene factor can be achieved after the leather has undergone several steps to make it resistant to decay and prevent rotting. The processes that leather undergoes put a stop to the inevitable decay that it would have experienced, was it not have gone through several chemical and physical processing.

-       Heat Conservation; leather serves as a mechanism through which the human body or the skin acts as a barrier against cold and other undesirable weather conditions. These insulation qualities made it an ideal candidate for early men to make use of leather during the cruel cold winter periods.

-       Environmental Sustainability; real leather does not have any harmful effects on the environment compared to the faux leather or other forms of synthetic leathers that are a product of the distillation of crude oil that pollutes the environment. They do not also undergo biodegradation, thus staying in the environment for hundreds of years while posing health hazards to man and other organisms. When natural leather is observed, it has no significant environmental or negative health impacts on man.

These unique features of leather that identify it as a premium material for craftwork, there are rules in place to guide against copycatting and other acts that try to pass off "fakes" as the real thing. Some statues and regulations make it compulsory that materials made from vegetable-tanned natural leather and those made from faux or synthetic leather by properly stamped or labeled indicating the type of material that it is made from. To ascertain the authenticity of the leather product that you are buying, most leather products have a stamp of originality on the material and showing that they do not contain harmful chemicals.

Classification of Leather

The classification criteria of leather are based on its current state of processing, and they are divided into three;

-   Finished; items made from leather that is sold both in physical stores and online are most times made from finished leather that has undergone all the steps of processing. This is to give the material a softer touch associated with leather, aesthetics, and other qualities that you would link with premium leather products.

-   Crust or Semi rough; here, the animal skin has gone through the initial stage of processing called tanning. Here the putrefaction that would have taken place had the leather not been treated would be halted considerably.

-   Fresh or Raw; the skin here has just been taken off from the animal and rubbed in salt, and it is yet to undergo any form of processing.

The animal skin can also be classified based on the section of the skin being processed, e.g., belly, side, back, etc.

Production of leather

From the finished leather product you have in your hands, you might assume that it underwent one or two steps to make it an ideal candidate for craftwork, you are wrong, very wrong. To get leather into that final finished state that makes it resistant, putrefaction free, soft, and have many other qualities that you look out for, it will go through not less than thirty-five stages. Most of these treatments are held in various facilities that are often hundreds of miles apart and sometimes in different countries. Some companies have developed highly specialized processes for the treatment of leather at multiple stages.

The type of treatment given to the leather is dependent on the unique nature of leather that the producer aims to have at the end of the whole treatment.

I will not bore you with the several highly specialized stages that leather goes through but will give you a detailed explanation of the significant steps involved in the tanning of leather.

Leather processing is the stages through which the material goes through from the raw, fresh state to the finished product, ready to be converted into highly-priced artifacts. The type of processing leather undergoes is dependent on the end-use of such leather. Let's take the case of straps or belts, here you will most likely be requiring a big thick leather, and on the other hand, if the leather will be used for furniture making, the leather ideally should be big and soft. Leather materials sued for clothing need to have qualities such as fineness, softness, and a generally pleasing appearance.

Vegetable leather or leather that has undergone vegetable tanning is the best candidate for almost any type of leatherwork. The peculiar nature of this type of leather makes it a craftsman's favorite. The soft and easily manipulated nature of the material makes it fun to work with.

The end use of leather hence differs a whole lot. For example, leather items to be used in cars, highly-priced fashion items, and household furniture are made of chrome-tanned leather materials due to the finished appearance and a standard outlook, which is more in tune with a large quantity of production. This is why it is essential that as a craftsperson, you pick the correct leather before you begin with any project.

Getting the Leather

The primary reason for rearing animals such as cow, oxen, alpaca, bison, etc. is their meat at least the majority of the time. Leather, bones are by-products. The animals are reared for the milk, source of transportation and beast of burdens in most societies, and the leather that is gotten from them is sold as an afterthought by the owner of the animal to the leather producer who sees it as a significant source of raw material for his business.

Preservation

This is an essential phase in the process, without which there will be no material to work with. It is the initial stage during which putrefaction and making the material stable is carried out, and this can be done in a variety of ways.

- The most important of these preservation methods is drying. Drying is carried out to get rid of the majority of the moisture content in the material. Drying can be carried out directly under the sun, but these methods only cry out the outer part of the skin because of the rapid rate at which the drying occurs. This discordant drying leaves the inner part of the skin still wet; thus, there is the likelihood of putrefaction again due to some moisture.

The skin can also undergo drying away from the sun's direct glare by placing it under some form of shade. This removes the uneven drying that happens when the skin is placed in direct sunlight. However, another problem arises the formation of folds and irregular shapes of the leather because the skin is not adequately stretched before and during the drying. To eliminate the difficulties faced in the first and second drying methods, the skin is stretched, making use of suitable materials such as sticks or metal rods before they are placed under a shade.

The skins all have different specific weights based on the method of drying that was employed. The weight is directly related to the amount of moisture content that the leather has at the end of the process. A fresh skin that is yet to undergo any form of processing is pegged at 100 (that is the green weight), skin dried directly under the sun = 85, skin dried under a shade = 80, skin dried under a shade with timber or steel frames used = 70.

The other way through which drying can be carried out is through the use of sodium chloride, commonly known as salt.

Listed below are other essential series of treatments that fresh animal skin is put through to make it stable enough to go through subsequent stages.

Soaking

This processing stage aims to return the skin to a state as close as the raw state before any treatment was carried out. The sodium chloride applied to the skin, and any other materials not wanted are taken out by rehydrating the skin in water. Surface-active substances, bactericides, alkalis, proteolytic enzymes, etc. are added to the water before the skin is immersed.

Hair removal and Liming

The application of lime softens the leather and enlarges the hair pores to make it easier for the material to readily take in the substances that will be used for tanning of the leather. This process is a two in one phase as the liming also takes out the hair from the surface of the leather and makes the skin pliable enough to receive and retain the tanning materials.

Splitting and Skiving

The skiving is done to remove any remnants of fat or flesh that is hanging onto the skin. On the other hand, splitting aims to smoothen the leather and remove uneven bumps to achieve a relatively even thickness. After the splitting of the leather that can be carried out immediately, the tanning is done with; the result is two types of materials which are the crust; lower layer, and the flower; the upper layer of leather.

Removal of Lime

Here the lime from the liming process is washed off the leather, pressed to remove the excess water, and gotten ready for the maceration stage.

Maceration

Here proteolytic enzymes are applied to the leather to bring about a loosening of the leather material.

Pickling

Here is the continuation of the removal of lime from the leather. The acid-base balance of the leather is returned to a level in which further processing can be carried out successfully.

Tanning

Here, the leather undergoes treatment with several substances such as zirconium, corm, aluminum, tannins, fats, aldehydes, etc. The incorporation of these substances into the structural composition of the leather is to make it strong enough so as not to be subject to the forces of environmental conditions such as moisture, chemical reaction, temperature, wear, and tear, etc.

The tanning process is an irreversible reaction on the leather, so there is no room for the deterioration of the leather components. The process of tanning can be carried out in a multitude of ways, which includes and is not limited to; the use of water combined with brains, fat, and oil that have undergone emulsification. The method of tanning leather using a bran mixture is a method that was used at the beginning of the preservation of leather by the early craftsmen. Nowadays, however, we have chrome tanning, which is a method making use of chrome ions that pushes out any water molecules in the collagen material of the leather for it to combine with the protein molecules present in the leather successfully. The end product is easy to handle and comfortable material that is a regular item in the clothing making with leather. Available are other specialty tanning methods; however, for that leather that you work on without breaking a sweat and getting from your neighborhood store, the vegetable-tanned leather is the go-to choice.

The term tanning was obtained from the chemical substances gotten from the exterior part of the plants called tannins. This method of using tanning or vegetable tanning is as old as man himself and has remained to this day because of the quality products gotten from the process. After the leather's tanning, it will still go through a few procedures to be ready for use.

The leather is composed of fibers with differing compactibility from the outer part of the skin, which is denser than the innermost part of the skin, which lies directly next to the meat or flesh. The end use of the leather will determine how the leather is divided into varying types based on whether the leather's inner or outer part is to be made use. The outer part of the skin is referred to as the grain, and the inner part is called the corium.

The full-grain type of leather comprises the outer part of the skin and the part between it and the corium. Typically, the grain has a tightly packed collection of fibers giving it a smooth and pleasing burnished outlook.

Moving away from the full-grain, the next type of leather in the hierarchy is the top grain type. This grade of leather is devoid of defects, scars, and other unwanted imprints in the skin that are removed by carrying out a shaving action on the level directly after the hair layer. With this level packed full of fibers eliminated, the longevity of this type of leather grade cannot be compared to that of the full-grain far outlives the top grain.

Finally, we have the last type of grade of leather, which is commonly known as "Genuine leather." It is typically located in the area where the corium begins; thus, it is made up of dispersed and unevenly distributed fibers. A common type of genuine leather is suede.

The rawhide is a category of leather that has not undergone tanning, and it is characteristically tough and cannot be easily manipulated. To work on it, it has to be soaked for a while in the water; it, however, returns to its previous state once the water dries off. This unique feather of this type of leather makes it useful in the construction of furniture, soles of certain types of shoes, drums, etc. Technically, rawhide is not categorized as leather because it hasn't undergone tanning.

Pressing, Splitting, Shaving

With the pressing action, the leather material undergoes compaction to remove as much moisture as possible that is remaining in the leather, and it also undergoes some drying. In the splitting stage, leathers that haven't undergone the treatment in previous phases are focused upon here or leather that are heavy. In the shaving stage, the thickness of the skin is reduced further to make the skin uniform's surface with no uneven bumps anywhere.

Tanning Again

This process is done over again, with the aim been to impact the leather desired qualities such as fullness and softness to aid the taking in and retention of essential materials that are applied to it during the process.

Dyeing

This gives you the choice of colors that can be given to the leather. However, the color can not just be applied to the leather without due consideration to the tanning mechanism that was carried out before. This is because the tanning plays a massive role in the type of color that can be applied to the leather at any given time.

Fattening

Here, substances such as oils from marine animals, mammals, or vegetable sources are applied to the leather to fatten it up, thereby improving their hydrophobic qualities.

After the fattening is done, the leather undergoes further drying to remove more water to the bare minimum, and staking is carried out. The staking is to make the skin soft and pliable. During all these processes, the skin will continue to enlarge in surface area, one of the ultimate goals of the processing.

Finishing

This is the final stage of the leather processing stages. Here the skins are put through several ever-changing mechanisms that aim to improve the looks and strength of the material. The color of the material can be altered by the addition of specific dyes and pigments. The surface of the skin can also be made to be more smoothened, or some form or wrinkles can be introduced to change the general appearance of the leather.

Chapter Two
Getting Familiar with Leather

The best known and readily available leather is from cattle, but you can also get your leather from almost any other animal ranging from snake to crocodile, fish to the ostrich, etc. Alongside the natural forms of leather, there are artificial types, e.g., polyurethane. With the numerous kinds of materials synonymous with leather, nothing beats the leather obtained from the cows' hides due to its unique ability to be dyed, stamped, carved, and tool.

The leather or skin used for the production of different materials are generally grouped into three categories;

- Hides, which are the skins of adult and matured animals such as the cow, horse, ox, etc.

- Kips, are the skin or outer coverings of the young of the animals listed in the previous group.

- The last group is the skin obtained from animals that are not as large as the cow, ox, horse, etc.

The type of skin most used in commercial activities is from cow, horse, deer, sheep, kips, etc. Nowadays, however, it is not uncommon to see products made from exotic animals such as snakes, reptiles, ostrich, etc.

For your practice sessions, you don't need to buy full-length pieces of leather; instead, you should go for scraps and irregularly shaped pieces of leather that will allow you to hone your skills. As you progress with your craft and begin to work on complicated and well-defined projects, you can then go shopping for more significant and regularly shaped leather. Typically, the skins of cows are not flat, and the different parts of the body have different levels of thickness, which means the ease with which these parts will be flattened differs. For example, the middle part of the leather is most times thicker and thin gradually as you move outwards.

The prices at which you get your leather depend on the apparent and inherent quality of the material. For example, buying a piece of the same part of leather can vary significantly based on the type of treatment the leather has undergone and where it is coming from. Qualities such as the extent and nature of tanning the leather are given, the type of cattle the leather was gotten from, how packed the grain on the leather is, scars, and other imperfections will affect the leather price.

For proper learning of leatherworks as a beginner, you should start with lower grades of leathers that might not necessarily produce pleasant results. High-grade leathers are most times quite expensive and will leave a massive dent in your bank account if you decide to make use of it in your practice runs. With constant practice on lower quality leather, you will, in no time, move onto been able to work on more expensive and high-grade leather.

Some folks who are conscious about the impact humans have on the environment try as much as they can to get sustainable materials for their projects. So what is done is that they go salvaging leather from a variety of sources. However, the challenge is that such leather obtained from such places can be a bit hard to work on. This is because the leather most times have undergone finishing making it difficult to dye or tool.

Do not despair if you fall into the categories of folks who love to recycle as there are several types of crafts that you can carry out with recycled leather. Recycled leather can be studded, snapped, and also conchos can be added to it. This is also in addition to cutting and sewing the material, which makes it ideal for individuals who are also careful about spending and saving the environment from unnecessary pressure.

Basic Leatherworking Activities and Tools

In this chapter, I will be taking you through the essential tools and activities that you will need to understand as a beginner with leatherworking. There is no fixed type of device or technique to be used as every individual will develop or series of processes to follow in achieving the result for a particular project, which may differ slightly or significantly from the next guy. For example, in sewing of leather, some folks are partial to hand sewing while others favor the sewing machine, and at the same time, others don't sew at all. What I will be touching on here are the barebones leatherworking methods and tools that can be built on and modified. The devices are not highly specialized, and at this stage, you will need to familiarize yourself with them before moving on to niche tools later on.

Leather Cutting or Removal

With leatherworking, you must inevitably carry out some cutting at one point or the other. To achieve this, there are different types of tools that can be put into action. With constant use, the tools used in cutting have to be honed appropriately for them to serve you well. If a tool is not looked after and maintained, the cutting of your leather will be a tiring and frustrating process resulting in badly cut material and waste of funds and time.

Scissors and Knives

A pair of well-honed scissors is a must-have that is used in cutting the needed pieces of leather from a more extensive stock. Scissors also come in the form of shears that are required for the effortless cutting of large hides. Shears give a much higher cutting pressure than the scissors, which is more useful for smaller cutting actions.

The Head Knife

The head knife is an all-rounder that can perform several tasks when the user knows how to use it correctly. It can be used to make small and detailed cuts and remove significant parts of leather from a whole section, skiving or beveling. The unique and distinctive design of the cutting part of the knife can be hard to get used to for beginners, but with constant practice and use, it will become a best friend that a leatherworker can't do without.

The head knife is also commonly referred to as the head knife when it is in the form of a larger and more curved type of head knife. The head knives are a dying breed, and you won't easily find them used in a lot of cutting processes save for some specialized functions.

Utility Knives

They are sometimes called snap-blade knives or box cutters used in removing small areas of leather at the edges. The sizes of these knives vary with the bigger ones ideal for removing or cutting leather with thick areas. These types of knives also do not pose a challenge in their maintenance.

Another type of cutting tool is the rotary knife, with the relative ease of use cutting a variety of lines ranging from curved to straight lines.

These are the basic types of knives that you will find in a typical leatherworker toolbox. However, there are many other types of knives, which are offshoots and modified variations of the ones detailed. The type of blade you eventually go with is that which you are most comfortable with and assured will give you the best results.

HINT: Any tool that has a sharp cutting edge or pointed needs to be handled with the utmost caution.

These tools that are bevels, cuts, gouges, or punches leather with relative ease will carry out the same action on your skin if proper attention is not paid to it.

Err on the side of caution in using any sharp tool as there is always someone out there staining the leather with crimson blood. If you are putting your children or any other young person through with leatherwork, watch over them, and ensure that only tools right for their ages are permitted to be used.

HINT: You must never use your metal hammer to beat on a metallic object directly. If you want to make use of your hammer, you can go for rubber or non-metal hammer that will not mar your material if the mallet you have at hand. However, it is a metal one, set up a piece of thick leather directly beneath the area that the punch is to be created to prevent the pointed part of the punch from going into the surface on which it is placed after the hole has been created the material.

The Rubber Head Mallet

The functions of a rubber mallet in leatherworking are numerous, and you will be amazed at how often you will reach out for it during a project. The creation of holes, stamping, embossing, the setting of dies, and rivets are best carried out with the aid of a rubber mallet. Some brands of rubber mallets have removable heads that give you the ability to change replace a defective head when it becomes unusable with the wooden or metal handle still very much functional. These types of mallets are very economical as there is no need to buy the complete unit. Instead, you continuously replace the head as needed.

When you go shopping for a mallet, you will come across various types, and your choice or hammering power you need is determined by your budget and other factors that are peculiar to you.

The Leather Awl

This is a ubiquitous piece of equipment that is to be found in any leatherworker's toolbox. This tool is made use of in the punching of holes needed in the marking of the leather for a design or stitching. As with other leatherworking tools, the awls are available in various sizes, replaceable or non-replaceable tips.

The typical awl has an elongated metallic part that broadens out as you progress away from the tip. The tip, when pressed firmly against the surface of the leather and pulled along the path of the proposed design, leaves behind an elegant outline that can then be worked upon by other tools.

Wooden Leather Burnishing Slicker

This is an essential tool that must be present in your toolbox if you aim to make quality leather works that turn heads. The burnisher is rubbed in a back and forth motion quickly over the leather, which generates heat and causes the leather's fibers to melt at the edges producing a gleaming finish. You can also get a burnisher fixed to a rotary device that quickly gets the work done.

Round Leather Stamping Mallet

This is not a must-have and is only used when you move onto stamping of your leatherworks. This stamping mallet has a slightly heavier weight when compared to the traditional mallet. This gives it a bit of extra pounding power. The circular rounded head is an advantage in the accuracy needed to get the precise spots. With the everyday use that the mallet will be involved in, the head's large area will be something that you will come to get used to and take advantage of.

Tooling Stamps

The numbers of leather tooling stamps are in the thousands, and you can rarely get all of them. The more you try to acquire a few, the urge to get the next set will always be there, and in the end, they will only take up the limited and valuable space in your box. Instead of continuously shopping for stamps, you can also produce your own to personalize your leatherwork from start to end. Simplicity is vital when it comes to buying and using leather stamps. You can always get a starter pack from the nearest store, and they come with a few necessary stamps that you can combine to give your work a great look.

Calipers

This tool is not an absolute necessity, but having it is a plus. Calipers are used for drawing uniform, even straight lines along the edges of the leather. When properly adjusted, the calipers can be used to mark the leather for other processes, such as grooving adequately. Besides drawing of lines, the calipers can also be used for decorative purposes by drawing fancy lines at selected places on the project.

Bone Folder Creasing Tool

In the molding of leather, this small tool is one guy that you should have in your corner. It is conveniently used in the molding of leatherworks such as a sword or knife sheath, holster, etc. to give that well-defined crease and edges to the piece. They come in a variety of sizes and shapes that are to be used for various leatherworks and not to forget, they are quite cheap, and won't put a dent in your bank account.

Adjustable Leather Stitching Groover

This implement is designed basically for giving an even and uniform marking to the edges of the leather and is has a part that can be adjusted in such a way to enlarge or reduce the coverage area of the tool. Some variants of this device have removable tips that can also be replaced with a blade if you need to make small cuts.

Sewing Thread

Leather threads are used in linking multiple pieces of leather pieces together. This is one of the several choices that you have for this process. You can make use of a temporary fix such as glue, but to be sure that the pieces will stick together, sewing is the best option. The type of thread to be used is determined by how strong you want the joint to be and how thick the leather pieces are.

Gouging and Grooving

In some projects, there is the need for a well-formed crease; thus, creating a bend is needed. To form this, a groove is cut on the underside of the leather to minimize the breadth of the leather to a thin line and, at the same time, gives a well-formed and clean bend just where you need it. The groove can also be cut on the upper side of the leather if there is going to be stitching involved.

The use of gouging tools such as the v-gouge and round gouge is an avenue through which fine and well-created lines can be repeatedly produced. The type of gouge that you use will determine how easy you find the project and the production of grooves. Gouges that the depths can be adjusted and lay straight on the leather's surface are the best to work with.

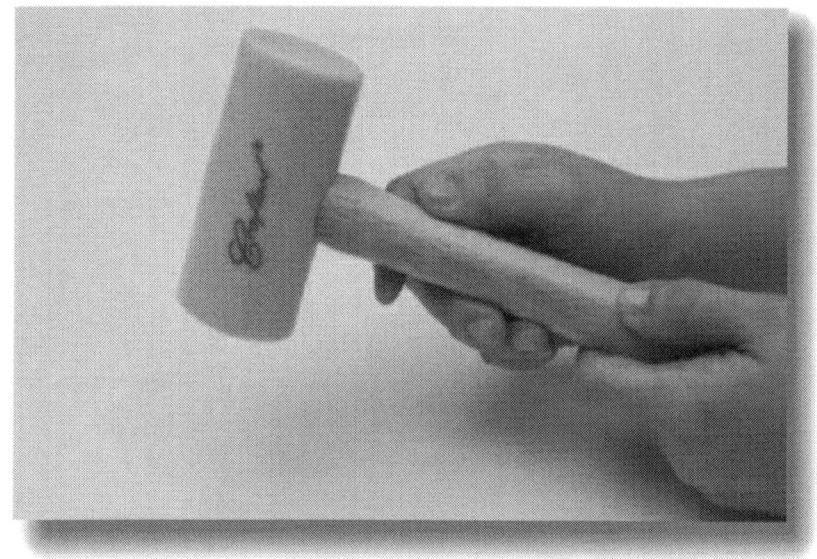

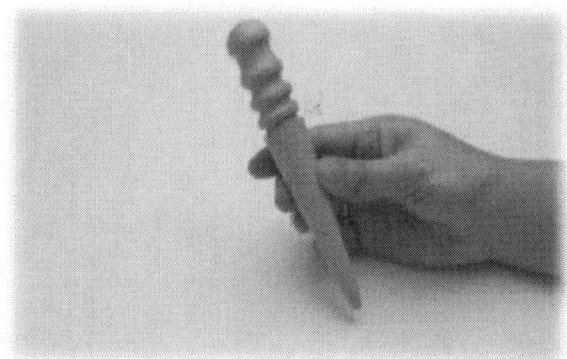

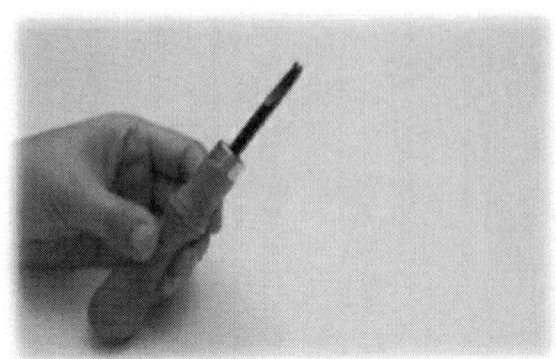

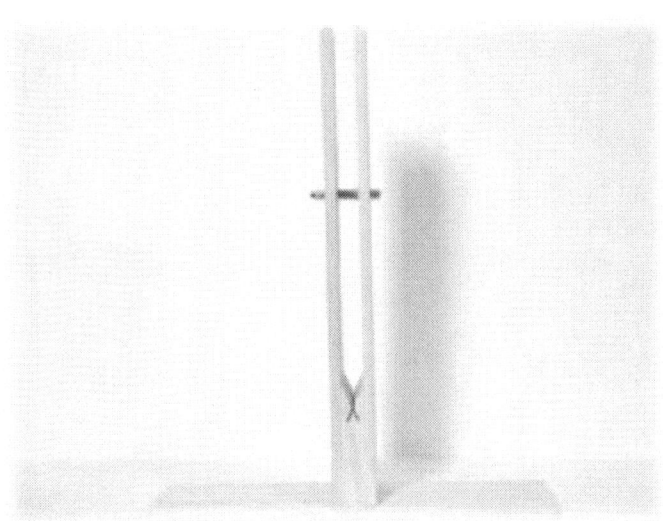

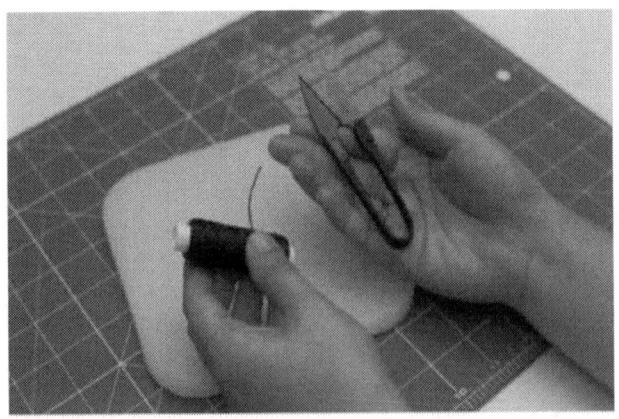

Swivel Knives

The embossing of designs onto the surface of leather requires the creation of lines with no depth at various areas on the pattern. The depth of these lines varies with different parts of the design, giving an illusion of solidity. With designs with circular and twisted patterns, you can bet that it will be hard to get it transferred to the leather surface with the aid of a straight cutting tool. To solve this problem, the blade is attached to a piece of equipment that swivels. It allows for easy alteration of movement and directions of the cutting point, giving you a seamless cutting experience of those curved patterns.

The swivel knife has a wide-angle with a sharp blade of thick proportions. The handle of the knife makes provisions to be guided by your pointing finger while at the same time held in a firm grip by the other fingers.

Edging and Beveling

There are several functions to which bevellers and edgers can be employed. Still, the most prominent is the removal of surplus or unwanted edges of leather through the process of beveling.

The same edger and beveller can be used for the same tool; though there is a slight difference in the cutting of the beveller, it produces an angled and flat edge while the edgers can either create a rounded or flat side. The cut produced along the edge of the leather varies in width, depending on the angle at which it is held. The actions of the tools are most times introduced to make it easier to bring several pieces of leather together and also to make the leather feel more comfortable against the skin.

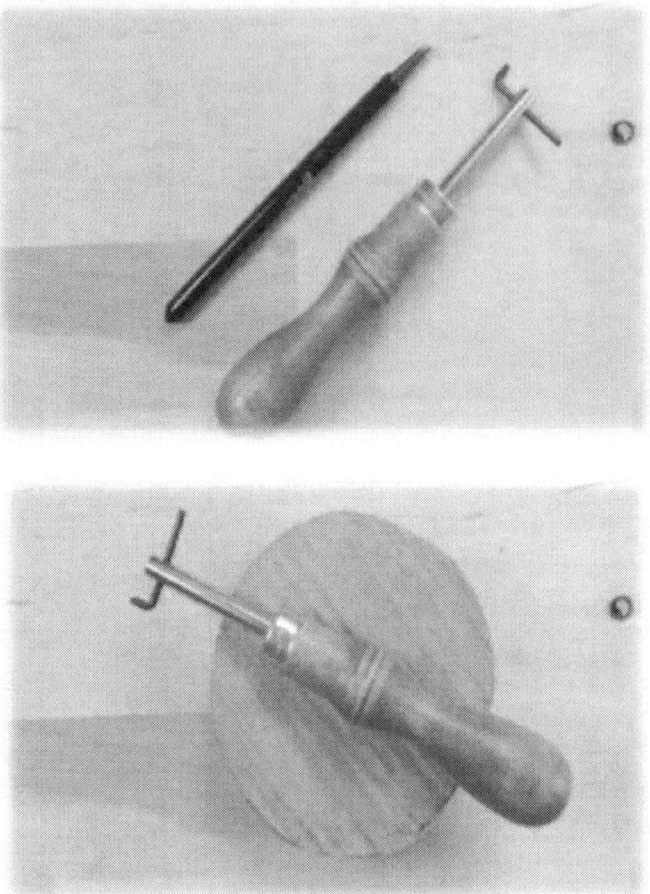

Punching

There are processes like the cutting of leather that involves detailed cutting of leather or the production of holes that are preferably carried out through the use of equipment with a sharp pointed end that punches the leather instead of cutting the material. There are accessories such as studs and rivets that typically need holes that are small or large enough to hold their shape. The major ways through which a punch can be performed is either through a stamp in which a die is beaten on leather, which has been placed on an anvil. The other way is called the squeeze method in which the punch pushes the die and the anvil on two sides.

Drive or stamp punch is used on heavy and thick leathers with several different types of designs. In addition to punching holes, they are also used to create shapes such as oblongs, ovals, and circles. As with all your tools, proper maintenance is essential, no matter the price paid for such a tool.

The other types of punches are the rotary or spring version, which allows you to move around several holes with different sizes and shapes quickly.

Joining Leather Pieces

When you have several pieces of leather that have been cut and are ready to move on to the next step of joining them, you can do this either by joining them permanently or temporarily. The permanent joining of leather is the focus of this section. The permanent joining methods include riveting, sewing, and stitching, while the use of clasps, Velcro, snaps can be used in the temporary arrangement. The technique of joining that you intend to use is determined by the nature of the project and the ease and advantages that such a joining method has over others. As a beginner, you might find it challenging to pick a joining method that will go well with the nature of the project at hand. This is where constant practicing comes in as you will be able to determine through trial and error the best approach to take.

Sewing

Hand sewing of leather is an ancient method of linking leather that has been in existence since man has fabricated and worn clothes on his back. The practice of stitching leather with hands is a practice that is very common among leatherworkers because of its ease and its adaptability to various situations. Sewing is a term best suited to cloth materials while stitching applies more to leather. However, both terms can be used interchangeably. In stitching, holes are prefabricated into the leather material through which the thread and needle are passed. With sewing, on the other hand, the needle passes through the cloth material and firmly drags the thread to hold the pieces of the cloths together.

In the formation of holes in the leather to be used for stitching, there are several types that you can use, and the basic ones are going to be touched here. The use of a machine is one aspect through which you can sew leather, but they have several restrictions that would inadvertently affect your work, such as the price and technical know-how needed to operate the machine.

However, if you started your leatherwork journey with hand stitching or you are a recent convert, you will be able to discern the difference in the ease of use between the two methods.

In stitching, the types of stitches available are as varied as the products on which they are used.

The type of stitch most favored by leatherworkers is the saddle stitch with several other types such as the baseball, hidden, and appliqué stitches.

Rivets, Grommets, and Screws

Some particular leather projects do not favor sewing as a method of joining leather, and you will have to seek out other means of getting your work completed while making sure that the functionality of the alternative means of leather joining does not in any way affect the aesthetics and usage of the leatherwork. As in stitching that makes use of holes already punched, makes use of hammered, bent or screwed metals.

Grommets serve basically to add strength to any part of the leatherwork that needs some backbone. The sizes of grommets on the market vary from the massive ones used on canopies and tarps to the relatively smaller ones used on clothing materials. A grommet on a leather material has a hole with a ring that allows a post to pass through on one side of the leather piece while on the other side, there is also a ring with the washer. The post on the opposing side is bent in such a way that it holds the washer from the other side firmly in position.

Though eyelets look a lot like the grommets, they have only a single ringed hole with a post. When the post is bent, it goes directly to the opposite side of the material. It should be noted that the grommet provides more strength to a linkage point than the eyelet. However, both the eyelet and the grommet both provide considerable upgrades in terms of longevity and looks of the final piece.

When a hole is punctured in a piece of leather and not adequately reinforced, constant use will ensure that it gets worn out faster than if it had been protected by the presence of the grommet or eyelet. These pieces of equipment are cheap, and it is better to have them installed on the leather piece than spending far more on repairing or replacing the piece later on.

Screws typically have two pieces that compliment each other; the female part has the thread on the inner part and the male head with the thread located on the outside. The male part is affixed to one part of the leather while the opposing leather will have the female screw situated there. The slight disadvantage with this method is that the screws can come undone when you least expect it to because of this downside, screws are used more for show rather than for any functional purposes.

Rivets are also not uniform, with them having various types that suites different project. The best-known rivet is the slender metallic rod in the shape of an umbrella. The majority of rivets on the market nowadays have one side flattened to enable the leatherworker peen a single end. The rivet post is typically pushed through a prefabricated hole on the leather material. On the other side of the piece, a washer is set up. The post is then edged in such a way that it can be pended to fix the washer down; thus, the connecting pieces of leather can be held down firmly. The preening of rivets is a skill and art that can only be improved through constant practice. If you don't want to use the rivets, there are other types of methods that you can use, but note that they are not as sturdy as the rivet linking technique.

The rapid rivet is a fan favorite in the world of leatherworking, and it is made up of a cap and base with a post. As is the tradition with other types of rivets, the post goes through the hole in the leather while the cap is then placed over the top. A compatible setting tool is placed over the cap and hammered to hold it firmly in place.

Another type of river is the tubular rivet, which is comprised of only one unit. When the post is pushed through the prefabricated hole to the opposite side, it is beaten down with a hammer or mallet's aid. The setting tool used in hold down the post divides the post into several slender pieces of metals, which you can then proceed to curve and pin to the leather. The attachment of these types of a rivet is easy to implement, but as it ages with constant use, the thin pieces of metals will most likely break away.

Needles

No matter the type of holes you have punched into your leather, at a point, you will need a suitable technique to insert a thread and secure the two pieces of leather together. There is a gulf of difference between the standard sewing needles and the leather sewing needles; they are much sturdier, and the pointed end is not that sharp when compared to the typical sewing needle. The leather needle's eye is also large enough to take in large thread types without giving you any trouble. Despite the relative advantage of the thick needle and the already fabricated holes, there is still the challenge of having broken needles once in a while when stitching leather. This is why you will need to buy a pack of the needle rather than in singles.

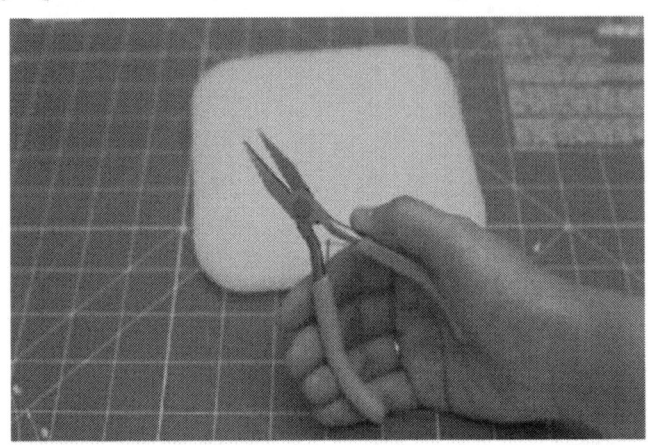

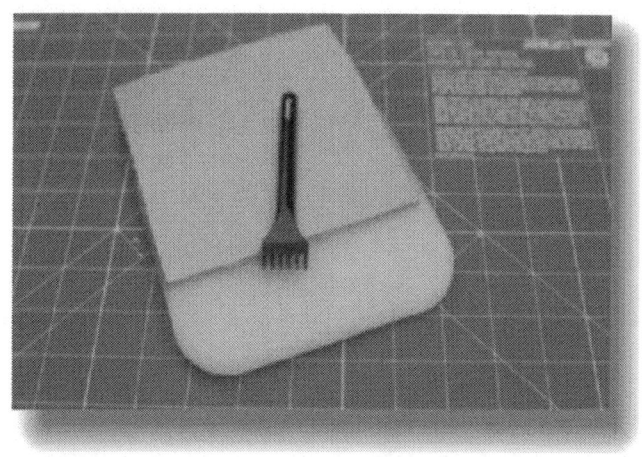

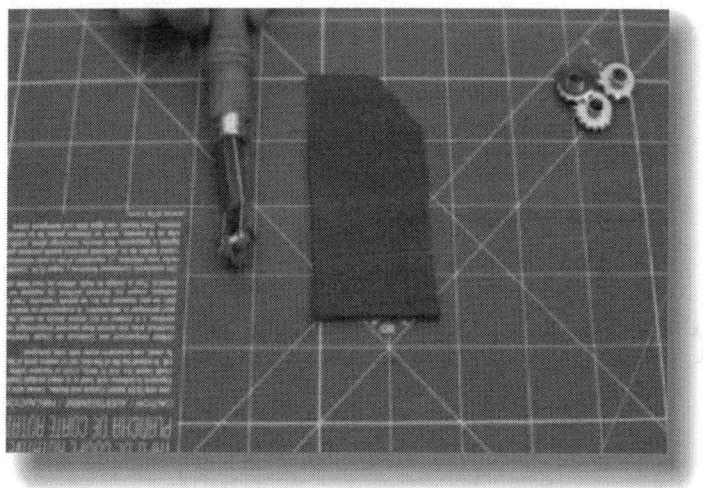

Closures

The type of closure that you choose to go with in a project will determine its functionality and ultimate durability. The cover chosen will be to be adequately secured to make sure that it performs optimally.

Rings and Buckles

For a leather strap used in a wristwatch, bag, belt, or some other clothing accessories, there are available different types of ways in which closure can be applied to secure the leather properly. For this type of leather piece, the most common ways of securing the leather are either to make use of a buckle with a straight and strong piece of metal to keep it firmly in place with the addition of appropriately punched holes or string the leather strap around a ring or pair of rings with enough force to keep it in place.

Buckles differ; there is the double bar, roller, the buckle with no mobile units, the center bar, two-prong, etc. With the vast array of designs, colors, sizes, etc., you are spoilt for choices on which type of buckle to go with.

With rings, however, there is the need to have the leather strap secured around them to hold the strap in place. Rings can come in the shape of a half-moon, spherical, circular, or some other shapes that will perform the task assigned well.

Studs and Buttons

Studs are a cyclical or spherical piece of closure material that is fixed to a short stem that has a foundation that employs a screw to lock onto the material. The hole through which the stud is passed is to have a diameter a bit reduced compared to that of the stud. The stud goes through the opening with the aid of the slit before it goes around the stem. The ease with which one opens and closes a piece of work having a stud as closure material makes it a favorite.

When you observe the leatherworks very closely around you, you will notice that many don't usually have buttons, as is the case with your typical clothes. However, if you want to include a button in your work, a unique style of button is referred to as the toggle button that will give your project an uplift. The button is cylindrically shaped and fixed at its center point. It moves in by the side, passing a loop and settles down properly. It does not come undone easily.

Snaps

You will love to have the snaps on your work because of the sound and feel you get directly from it as clicks into place. With a hand, you can push it into place and open it, and they don't come undone by mistake, which can lead to a wardrobe malfunction. A typical snap needs to have an opening the leather for it to go through. The topmost part of the stud links to the socket and the cap while the lower end is fixed to by the eyelet.

Clasps and Hooks

They bear a lot of similarities with buckles with clasps coming in the form of plastics, bone, or metal. They are often in the form of two intertwined units, but you can still get single unit types. The strength with which the clasp secures an enclosure differs, so the type of project to be done will determine the type of fastener to be used.

Glue

This material has been in use in the leatherwork industry for a long time and continues to serve as a crucial joining material. Types of glues include and are not limited to; super glue, rubber cement, etc. Glues can serve temporary purposes when other actions are being carried out on the leather such as sewing, or permanent fixtures in the design. With the vast array of leather, you will have to play with different types to determine which will go best with your leatherworking projects at any stage. Other factors to consider are how strong the glue is and how long it holds, is the smell agreeable with you?

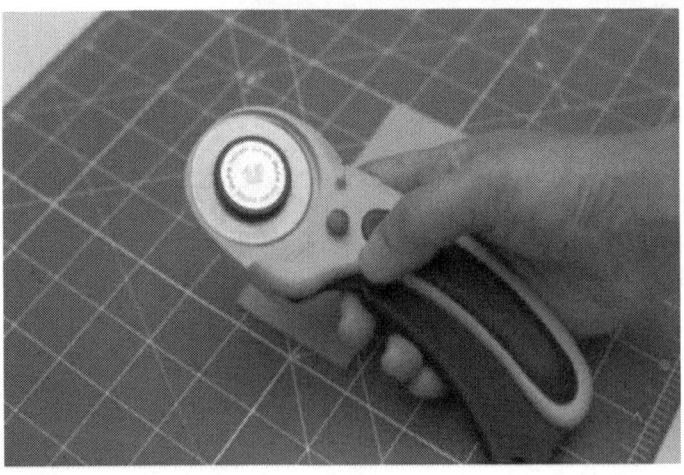

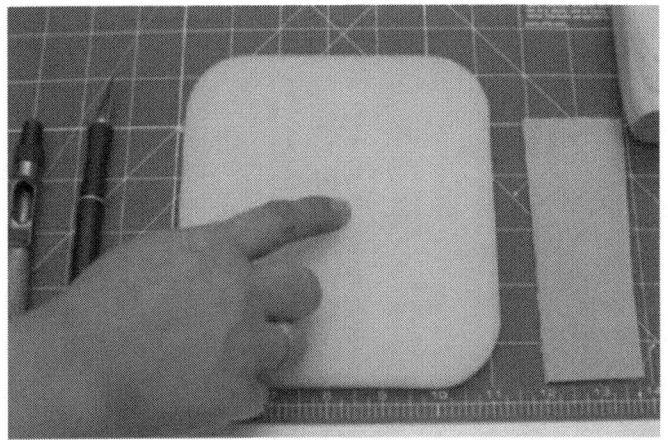

Magnets

Magnets used in leather project closures can either be fixed to the leather through the aid of thin metal spikes or sown directly onto the leather surface. The major disadvantage of using magnets as closure agents is that they can quickly come undone, but they are favorably looked upon for the ease with which they close. In some projects, the magnets are used as a second closure option and a significant closure device.

Chapter Three
Decorating and Shaping your Leather

The starting point for how your leather project will turn out starts from the design pattern you have in mind, how you cut and join in. Other ways in which the beauty of your project can be brought out include and are not limited to stoning it with rhinestones, decorative cuttings, etc.

Conchos and Spots

Conchos are a great way through which you can beautify your work. These materials have a form of attachment, which can either be a rivet or a screw through which it is held firmly to the leather. Other than riveting or screwing, the conchos can also be tied to the leather.

On the other hand, spots can be referred to as studs and are either metallic or plastic. You will find them on the jackets or bikers and in other niche designs. There are tiny metal spikes at the back of the studs or screws used in attaching them to the leather.

Carving

When you hear the word carving, wood comes to mind, cutting, and removing parts. In leather, however, carving or tooling does not in any way relate to this. Instead carving of leather is a sequential action used on leather to get some desired properties and qualities from the processed material through manual means. Tooling, which is a process of stamping or embossing of leather is most times, carries out alongside with the carving process of can be done on its own.

The equipment used in the carving of leather can be found in other forms of art crafting, such as pottery. A regular set of carving tools can form lines, sharp angles with corners, smoothen the leather, form depressions, and other tooling functions. The carving tools are best used alongside other leatherworking tools in other to create pieces worthy of your skill set.

Molding

Leather can be molded into almost any shape or design when it is wet, and the shape that has been created will still maintain that particular design after it has dried out. Molding of leather need not be a hard task as it does not have any specific tool that you should have. All that is needed to get the molding process started is an object with the same shape as the case or package that you want to produce. For example, if you're going to create a sheath for a knife, you can use an existing sheath or other materials with the same shape as the knife. If the object that is to have a case created for is water sensitive such as a phone, it is unlikely that you will wrap a wet leather around the phone to get a mold for it and wait for it to dry out. To get around such a situation, you can use a 3D printer to get the exact shape of the phone or tablet and then wrap the wet leather around the model. The formation of sharp angles, corners that will most likely be needed in the molding is best done with tools such as the plastic, bone, sanded wood, etc.

To ensure that there is as minimal movement as possible, the wet leather can be firmly held down in the desired position with appropriate pins' aid. Not all pins are desirable as they can cause discoloration of the end product, e.g., iron nails, clips, or tacks. To prevent this from happening, use plastic or wooden pins or clips. The clips or pins to be used should also have the jaws wrapped in soft, thin leather to guide against the transfer of the jaw marks to the leather.

Hand Stitching Leather

Leatherworking involves a plethora of skills that you may or may not need in your everyday crafting. There are necessary skills that are an essential part of your journey that won't cost you much, and the time spent learning them will appear in your works in the future. One such is skill is leather stitching. This section is dedicated to showing you how to go about hand sewing leather using one of the most durable stitching techniques.

Sewing leather manually is a cost-effective, time management, and cheap way of stitching leather. The technique we will be touching on here is the saddle stitch method. One crucial fact that a lot of leatherworkers and purchasers of leatherworks fail to appreciate is that hand-sewn pieces are one of the most durable and long-lasting pieces that you can ever buy with your money. When compared to machine stitches, which, if it breaks, there is no stopping of the whole threadwork from coming undone, the hand stitch, however, on the other hand, will have the threads hold other threads together if breakage occurs.

- To carry out a saddle stitch, a pair of needles will be needed, and on opposite ends of the thread, a needle will be fixed. The thread used for leatherwork is unlike the type used for regular clothing stitching; it is much more reliable with heft and typically has several cords of individual synthetic threads intertwined.

- First, unroll about 3 feet of the thread, or you might need more depending on the project requirements. Thread one meets at one of the ends and then insert the needle into the thread once or twice about 4cm from the end.
- Draw the thread till it goes past the eye of the needle before securing it. Apply some beeswax at the area where the insertion was made on the thread and gently roll it with your fingers. Carry out the same process at the other end of the thread with the remaining needle.
- Move to the leather and produce a line that is the replica in length from the boundaries of the leather material compared to how thick the leather pieces joined together.
- Space in-between holes fabricated depends on how thick the leather is, the heft, and the leather's end-use. With the use of an awl, to pinpoint and mark the areas to be worked on precisely, an overstitch wheel is the best tool to engage. You can also make use of a chisel fork in place of an awl; the choice is yours.
- Set the leather pieces in the alignment of how the will be stitched. On a table with no dirt or any other unwanted material, lay a thick piece of leather that will serve as protection for the work. The leather should be one that can be damaged without you getting antsy.
- Set up the chisel fork on the previously marked points and gently use a rubber head mallet to beat it on the leather. The fork should penetrate both pieces of leather and come out on the other side.
- Remove the fork and move onto the next site. Continue with the punching until all the entire length of the leather has been worked on.

The name saddle stitch came from the technique of holding the leather on a saddle-like device while stitching. In the end, the leather been sewn should be held with any device as long as you have your hands free and able to work without any hindrance. Securing the leather is all up to you as long as the needle goes through the first hole and moves through the other hole until it gets to the center of the thread.

- Pick up one of the needles that will go through the rear side of the project and thread it through the punched hole that is nearest to you.

The stitching is to be done coming towards you.

- Thread in about 3cm of thread in the hole. Pick the needle laying at the front side and insert the pointed end into the hole at the foreside of the thread been inserted. The method with this technique of stitching is to always place the needle on the foreside in front of the thread of the needle on the rear side.

- When you are about to thread in the needle on the foreside into the hole, check thoroughly to ensure that the needle does not touch or go through the thread coming in. If an accident occurs and the needle touches or goes through the thread, the whole operation will have to be canceled and restarted. To prevent this from happening, the thread coming should be pulled back as the needle comes in from the front. As the needle from the front gets in halfway, the pulling can stop, the two needles are handled, and the stitch is pulled to firm up.

This same procedure should be carried out for all the other holes, and in finishing the threading, a backstitch will be done on the last pair of holes. This implies that an alteration of the direction will be carried out for the penultimate and last stitch.

Passing in the needle into holes that already have threads will be tough. To get through this stage, you can make use of needle-nose pliers to pull in the needle. As you pull in the needle at this point, exercise the utmost caution to prevent the needle's breakage.

When the last stitch is done, cut the thread next to the surface of the leather.

Before the stitching begins, you might decide to create a gouge between the holes for the thread to settle in when you are done with the stitching. This is a way through which the longevity of the stitch and the piece can be ensured.

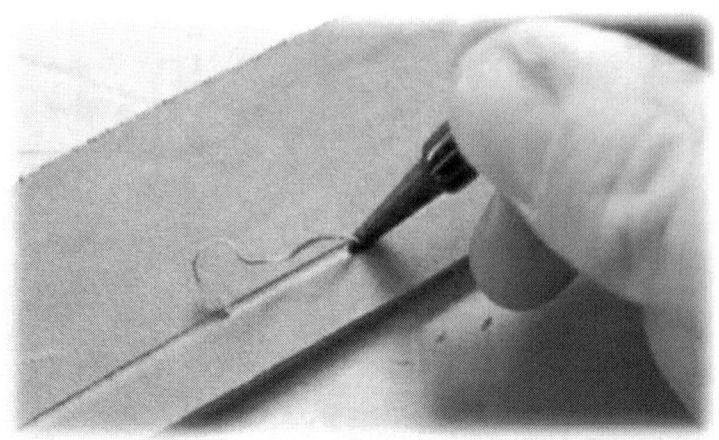

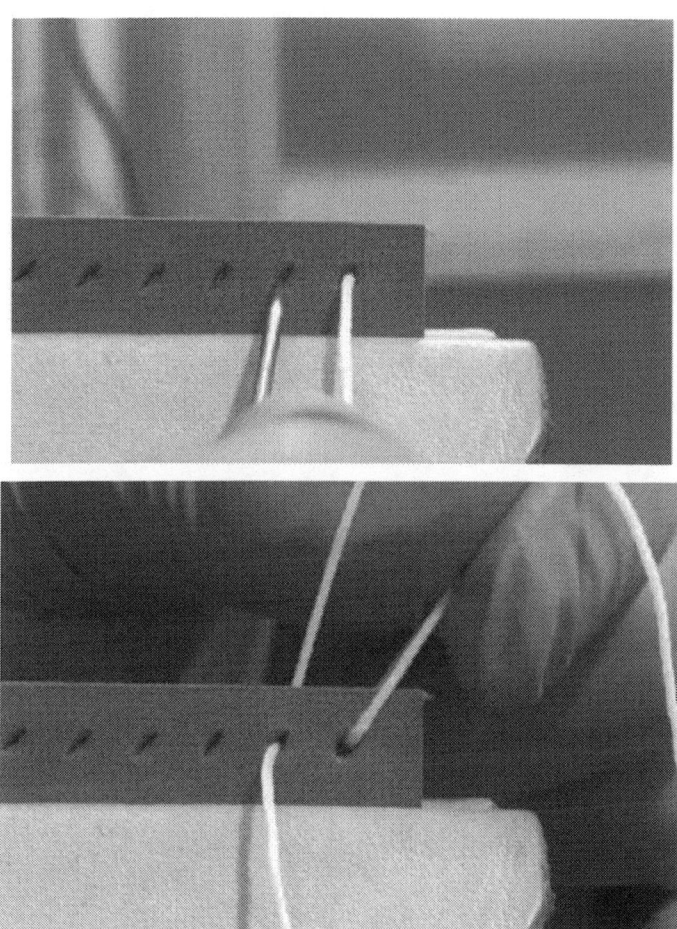

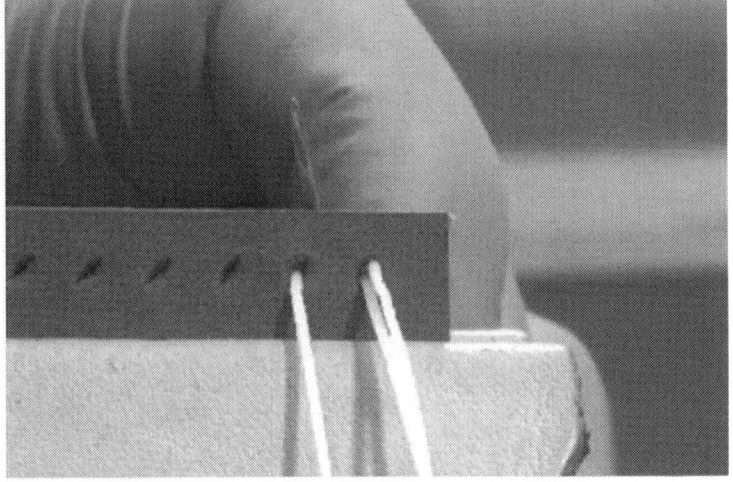

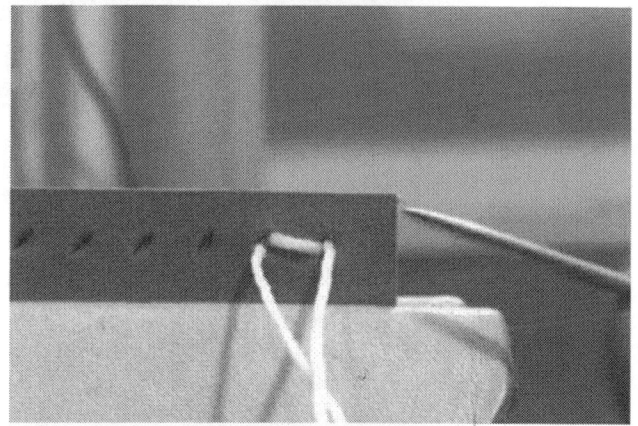

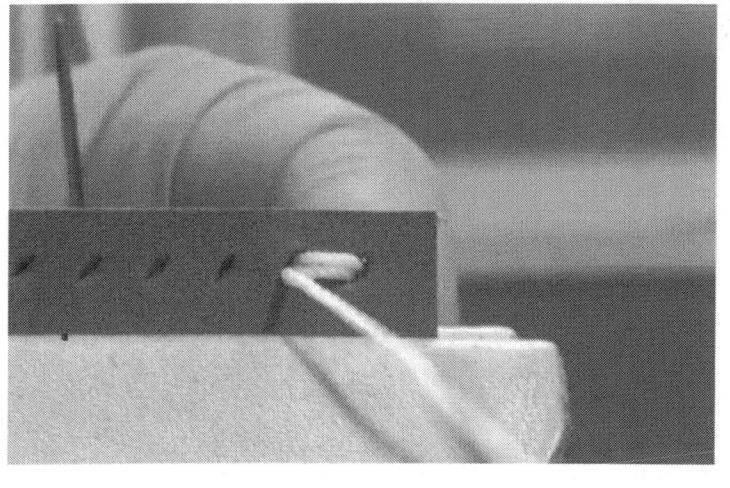

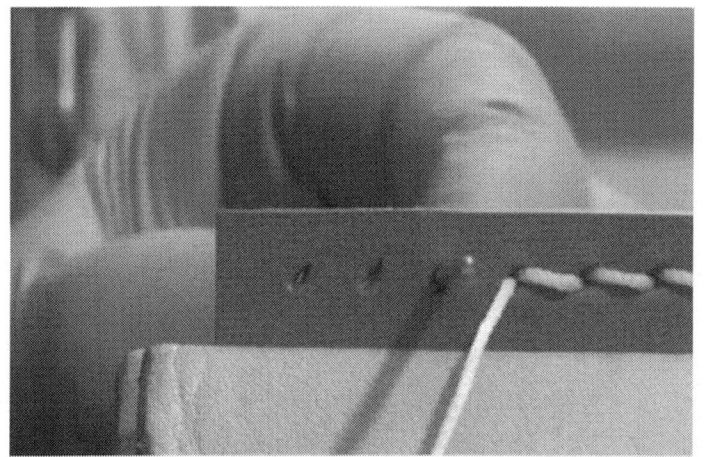

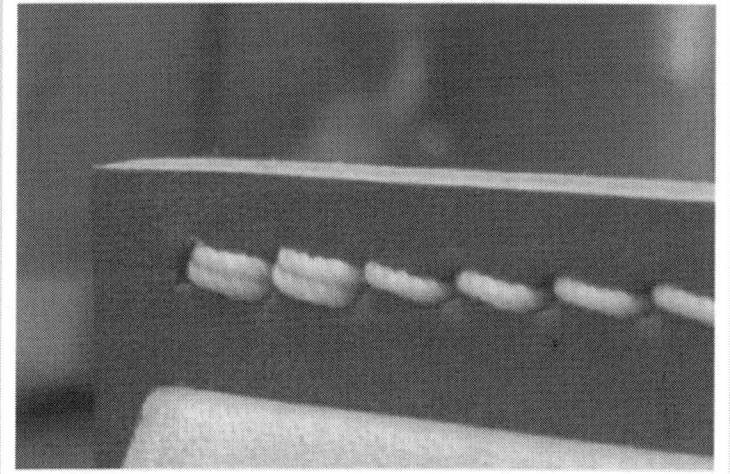

Wet Forming Leather

With this type of treatment that leather undergoes, two primary methods are commonly used, and they are; using a two-piece mold and manually. Any of the ways that you decide to use will require some strength as they can be energy demanding. The two-piece mold method is ideal for items that will be seeing a lot of use while the hand forming method is best suited for items that will rarely be used.

The best type of leather for wet forming is the tanned vegetable leather, and it is best to use leather that is strong and firm because they tend to maintain the formed shaped perfectly. However, you can also use certain medium or soft leathers as long as they keep the shape without much hassle.

What you should look out for is how thick the leather is, because this will affect how easy it will be for you to fix it around the mold. The thicker the leather, the more time and experience you will have to apply to get the molding done. Leathers without much thickness are a beauty to mold, and this is the best type of leather that beginners should start with.

Manual Wet Forming

Even though the two methods of wet forming require a lot of strength to get done, this method on its own is more energy-consuming. After several attempts, when I started working with leather, I discovered that the 5oz+ leather is not ideal for manual wet forming most times if the subject has a bit of height. If you are working with smaller objects such as a single pen case, it is a great leather to work with. However, if a bag is the case, you will be facing a lot of challenges. This is because a bag pattern will need a more significant mold, and if you decide to go ahead with it, it will probably be an exercise in futility and may not be worth the stress you put yourself through. Here are the steps to get you started;

- The first step is to cut out the amount of leather needed to cover the mold without having too much surplus sufficiently or not having enough to cover it. Ideally, it is best to have a little surplus leather covering the mold that will work best. This can be a bit tricky, gauging the perfect amount of leather needed to thoroughly cover the mold or shape you are working on. To be on the safe side, always give room for some excess, place it on the mold or the object, and cut the needed leather with room for surplus. Remove some of the surpluses as this will lower the probability of wrinkles that will be formed when the forming starts and reduce the size of the lines that will come up. In essence, this will save you a lot of working and fighting with the leather as you try to mold it.

- The next step is soaking the leather, and you can accelerate the process by using your hands to press and pummel the water and leather mixture; focus more on the rear end of the leather. The leather should be allowed to sit in the water for about forty-five minutes before taking it out and working on it.

- Take out the leather from the water and place it over the mold or object and firmly fix it with your hands. Focus more on the edges and curves that define the general outline of the object. Continue with this until the leather takes on the shape of the mold. After this, set the mold and the leather down on a flat wooden board and clamp down the leather on the surface. Move on to firming up the leather around the sharp edges and corners with a bone folder. Begin from the topmost part of the mold and proceed towards the bottom. There will be the formation of air pockets as you do this. When you get to the lowest part of the mold, raise the clamp and tighten the leather by pulling it down a bit more over the mold before fixing the clamp back to the surface of the wood. Do this several times until you are satisfied with how it looks.

HINTS: the wet forming process can go on longer than you envisioned, and during this time, the moisture content of the leather will start to reduce, causing it to become tougher to work with. To solve this, always have some water and a piece of soft foam at hand to rehydrate the leather as you work.

A piece of wet leather is prone to accidents such as marks that you can inflict on it, which is not part of the original concept that you have in mind. To get this sorted, pick up a spoon and firmly press the curved portion in a circular motion over the affected part to regain its original appearance.

The formation of curves and sharp edges can be a headache when working with wet leather. Working on the smooth or flat surface is a breeze, but once you move onto an angle, the likelihood that the leather will begin to fold or bunch is increased. To overcome this problem, the cut of the leather should be as close to the mold surface as possible. Predicting how much leather is required for a wet forming can be difficult, so leave about two inches around the edge when working with an object and about one inch when a mold is used.

When the project been wet formed has a depression, bunches will unwanted folds will start to develop as you mold. To solve this problem, cut where the bunches are, from the bottom of the object out to form a triangular cut. Typically, there will be several of these cuts on the edges, and you will have to get a flattened object to place over these areas. The cut's essence is to allow the leather to expand out rather than folding or bunching up.

When using a mold rather than an object, go with the following steps;

- Cut the amount of leather needed.
- Soak the leather for the required amount of time.
- Form the leather around the mold and remove any surplus from the edges, leaving about an inch.
- Press down the leather at the top of the frame and firmly hold it down with a clamp-on a wooden board's surface. Make the triangular cuts at the folds and bunches. Let the leather and the mold sit for one day.

So how do you go about the creation of a mold for your subject? Here is a quick guide on that.

The mold is made of two integral parts, which are the frame and the form. The form is the object on which the leather is placed, while the frame is the material that you force down on the leather on the form.

The form can be a piece of flat wood onto which smaller pieces of wood are fixed, usually having the general shape of the object. Work on the pieces of wood to be smoothened without any unwanted corners or curves.

The frame is formed in a general shape that will fit over the form.

It is always essential that you consider the thickness of the leather be worked on when constructing the frame and the form. The mold must have the appropriate width and length in addition to the depth of the leather, while the form should have the needed breadth and length without the thickness of the leather included.

Here are a few tips;

- Make use of hardwood when constructing the frame and form.
- Ensure that the frame is as tight as possible.
- Always use G-Clamps and nothing else.

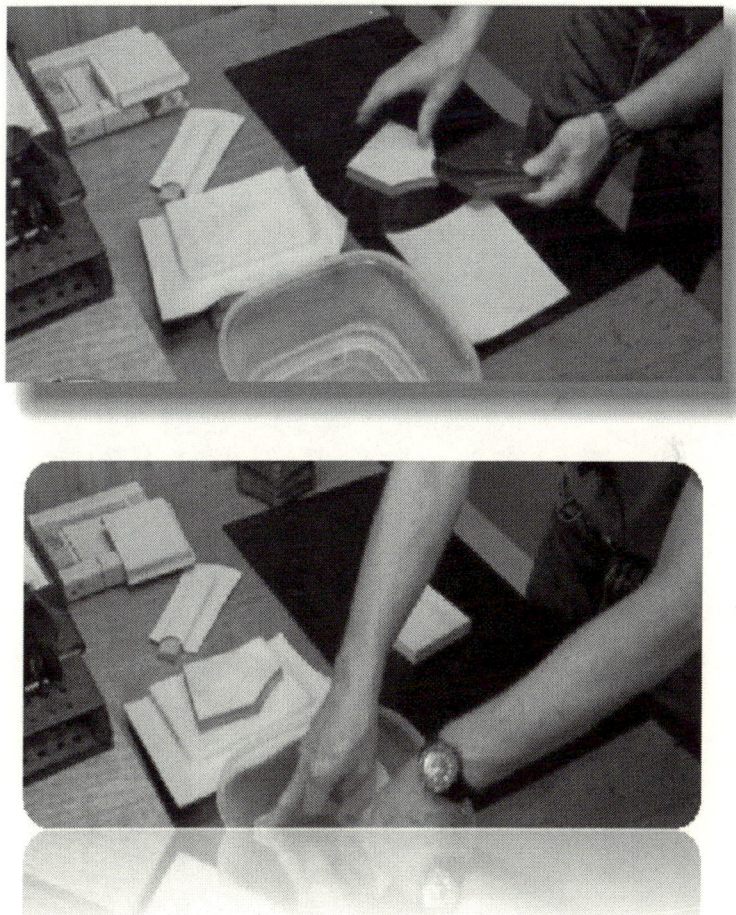

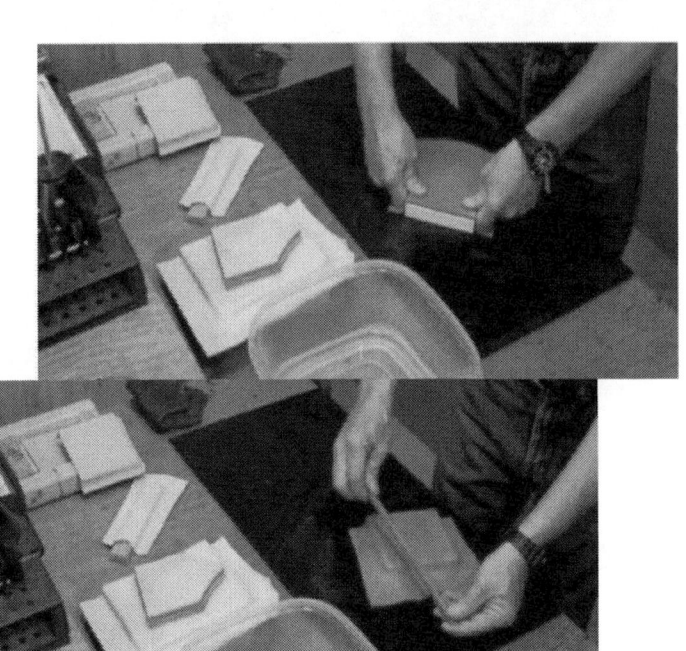

Straightening Wrinkled Leather

Leather can be a hard material to work with, and its wrinkling comes naturally or when treated with some chemicals, and this most times is not a wanted quality as it affects the appearance of the finished product. To get the wrinkles out of your leather; you will require the following supplies;

Cloth rags

Iron

Blow dryer

Directions

- Hang the leather in the bathroom when you have a hot bath or shower. This enables the leather to be adequately steamed.

- After the steaming is done, place the leather on an ironing board or any other flat surface.

- Massage the leather with your hands and try to remove as many wrinkles as you can with your hands.

- Arrange some clothes on the rag, put on your iron and press it over the cloth.

- Apply the blow dryer over the areas with the wrinkles.

- Do not allow the hot iron or the dryer to come in direct contact with the leather.

- When you are done treating it with the blow dryer, you can apply some mild soap to the surface with a damp cloth. After this, sprinkle and rub some baby powder over it. This is to block the pores on the surface of the leather and give it a shiny gleam.

Shrinking Leather with Alcohol

The factors that bring about the shrinking of the leather vary, and hot water is one of the most common ways to achieve this. To ensure that the desired results are achieved using hot water, a rubdown with alcohol must be carried out. The application of alcohol removes the hydrophobic layer guarding the leather against the action of water. This allows hot water to penetrate the leather properly. The combination of alcohol and water is the best way to bring about the shrinking of leather other than the use of hot water. The shrinking process can be carried out several times but note that the leather will not undergo any reduction in size after the first shrinking process.

To carry out a shrinking or leather, the following supplies will be required;
Leather
Rubbing alcohol
Leather conditioner
Bucket
A piece of cloth

Directions

- To a bucket, add equal parts of alcohol and water to the midway point of the bucket.
- Dip the leather into the bucket and allow it to sit there for about fifteen minutes.
- Take out the leather from the mixture. Wash the leather with some water and squeeze to remove any remaining water.
- Set up the leather outdoors under a shade in an airy place for at least a day.
- Apply some conditioner with a piece of cloth to the leather. This acts as a process of returning the hydrophobic qualities that the alcohol removed from it. Rub the conditioner into the leather with gentle and round motions. Allow the leather to air dry again for another day before applying another layer of conditioner to it, and then it is good and ready for use.

Setting Crystals in Leather

With the soft and bendable surface of leather, you are given an avenue through which you can decorate and bring out the beauty of leather through the addition of crystals and stones to your pieces. In other materials, before crystals and stones are added to the surface, it will first be set in stone before attaching it to the surface. With leather on the other hand, however, you can get to set the crystals or stones directly to the leather surface.

Materials

A small craft knife

Leather

Leather cement

Water

Crystals

Directions

- Soak the leather in cold water for about ten to fifteen minutes. The duration of soaking will differ, and this is based on how thick the leather is. The thicker the leather, the longer the time that it will need to be sufficiently soaked.

- Take out the leather from the water and allow all the excess water drain from it, but it should still be soft and damp enough to work with.

- With the craft knife, make a small cutting that is the shape of the stone you intend to set there. The cutting should be on the leather's surface and should be shallow and should not be deep as to cut through the leather to the other side. With this in mind, you should make use of thick leather so that you don't damage the leather while trying to cut a space for the stone. However, if you still want to make use of thin leather, you should omit this stage.

- Set the stone into the cut and firmly enclose the leather around the stone with your fingers ensuring that the leather encircles the crystal to keep it securely and place and prevent it from falling off.

- With the stone set in the leather, drop the leather with the area having the stone in boiling water and let it stay there for about twenty seconds. Remove the leather with the stone still firmly wrapped by the leather until the leather cools down considerably. The part of the leather having the stone set in the leather should be the only part allowed to come in contact with the hot water.

- Take the stone from the leather while it is still damp and into the cut in the leather, add some drops of leather cement, and do the same for the lower part of the stone. Set the stone into space and secure it firmly with a piece of twine.

- Set the leather with the stones in an airy place and allow drying for at least twelve hours.

- Cut out the twine and unwrap the leather. The stone will have been fixed into the space with the leather cement's aid and the hardening of the leather.

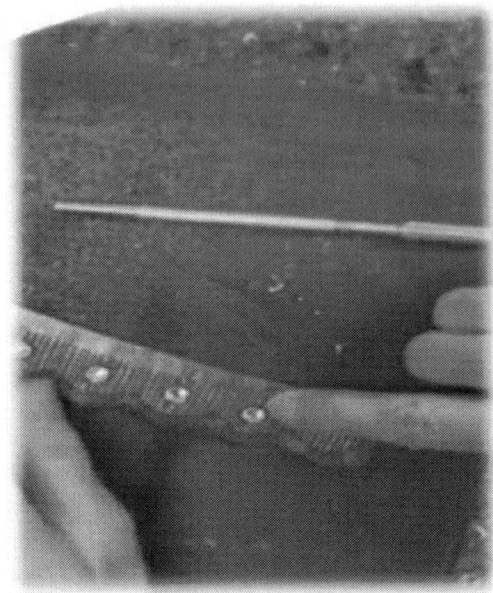

Writing on Leather

Writing can not only be done on paper or cardboard, but leather is also a perfect surface to be written on. It readily accepts many different actions, such as dyeing due to its breathable and robust nature. Materials needed to write on leather are;

Marker or leather pen
Ruler
Cardboard
Chalk

Directions

- Set up the cardboard on a clean and flat wooden surface.
- Take off the covering on the leather pen after shaking it for a few seconds.
- Write out what you intend to transfer on the cardboard with the pen or marker.
- Place the leather on a table and create lines with chalk on the leather to ensure that the writing will stand upright if that's your intention.
- The leather should be held firmly with your hand or a clamp while you write the exact words on the cardboard earlier.

- The writings should be allowed to sit and dry for about sixty minutes.

Embossing Leather

This is a stage in the leather production process in which specified tools are used to emboss patterns, logo, designs, or any other unique additions to the leather's surface. Tools such as sliders, rollers, metal plates, etc. are used. Some leatherworkers also make use of hot stamping tools on vegetable-tanned leathers. Stamping on leather is a way through which one can get to personalize that particular leather piece. Initials, brands, dates, quotes, symbols, and many other things can be embossed on the leather.

If the tools needed for embossing on leather are not readily available, you can use a clamping technique. Note that embossing is not carried out on leather that has undergone pre-treatment only on unfinished leather. The stamps can be bought from your neighborhood hardware store or ordered online. A metal charm can also be used but ensure that it does not have a tapered pattern but should have cut edges. This is to make the design on the leather stand out and more distinct.

- Set up the leather are to be embossed on a table with the backside of the leather lying directly on the table. The edge of the leather should be as close as possible to the edge of the table to enable you to secure it with a clamp.
- Using a wet sponge, gently rub it over the surface of the leather. The leather should be damp and not dripping with water.
- Set up the embossing tool, which can be a metal stamp over the leather at the area where you want the design imprinted.
- Place the C- clamp on the middle part of the stamp and turn it until you can't turn it again. Let the clamp remain in that position with the metal stamp for about thirty minutes before removing it.
- Apply some leather finish to the embossed surface to ensure the longevity of the area. This should be carried out before any other processing, such as sewing or joining different parts of the leather piece.

Leather Stamping

As discussed earlier, the range and complexity of the type of stamps used in leatherworks are mind-boggling. You can make your stamps from the cap of screws, studs, etc. or buy insanely expensive top of the line stamps. The stamps' patterns or designs are easily recreated on endless pieces of leather by using a single stamp or by being ingenious with several types of stamps on a single piece of leather to produce unique designs. Do not forget when stamping not to use a metallic mallet or hammer. Your workspace and, most importantly, the table on which the stamping is to be done should be devoid of any foreign materials that will impair the stamping process's outcome.

Buy your stamping set from any retailer closest to you or order online. A 3D stamp is a good option as it comes with a cylinder that can be fixed with several stamps at any given time. When buying, ensure that the stamps and the barrel are compatible. The cylinder is the tool that is to be employed when beating the pattern of the stamp onto the leather material.
The leather should have the backside resting directly on the table, and the front side should be facing upwards.

-    Pick a location on the unfinished leather surface where the design will be located.
-    Dampen the surface with a sponge and then place the stamp over that area.
-    Fix the stamp into the cylinder and secure it properly with your hand.
-    Pick up a rubber head or wooden mallet and pound it a few times while ensuring that the stamp does not change position.
-    After several poundings, remove the stamp to view the new pattern created on the leather. If the imprint is ok, then the work is done and, if not, carefully set back the stamp into the pattern and beat it again.
-    If you have other stamps that you want to use on the same leather, carry out the same process, after which you apply a leather finish to the surface.

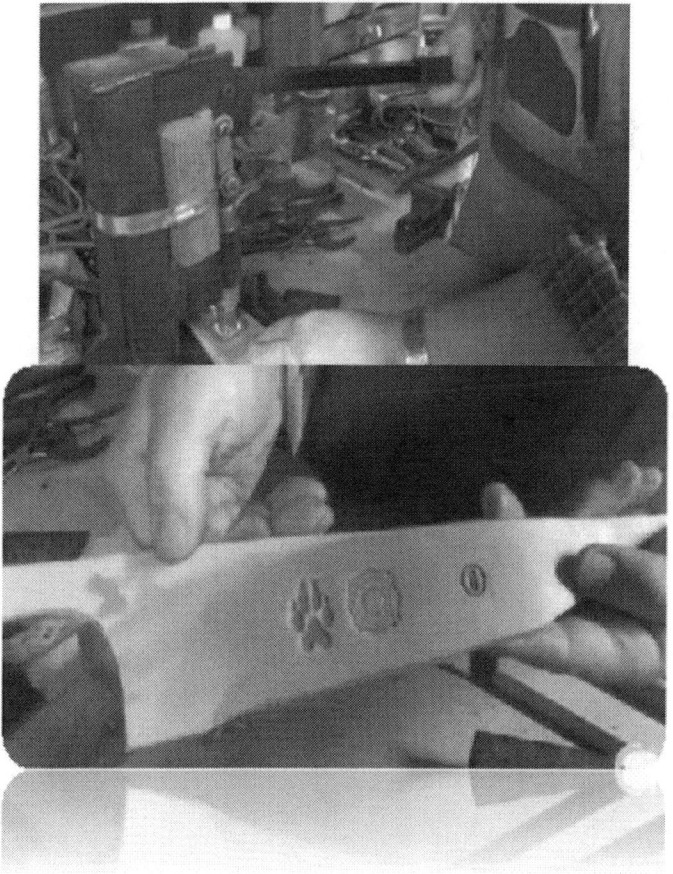

Elementary Leather Carving Method

The type and intricate carving designs applied to a leather piece depend entirely on the leather piece's nature. For example, a book and a small purse have the size and shape for them to have designs that can bring close enough to view and check out the smallest details. With larger projects such as a sign, belt, jacket, etc., there might not be a need to input as many details as with the smaller objects. The smaller objects will require more time to finish because of the painstaking amount of time needed to input and carve all the details. With large projects, just a fraction of the time is required to get the work done. The type of details you decide to put on your piece is determined by the quality, what the piece is to be used for, etc.

In carving leather, go with the following steps;
- Get a piece of vegetable tanned leather, stay away from leather that has undergone chrome tanning because it won't hold onto patterns carved into it.
- Draw or transfer the design you have in mind onto a waterproof piece of paper.
- Use a damp sponge to rub down both sides of the leather without allowing the water to be too much on the leather.
- Place the waterproof paper with the drawing on the leather and secure it with masking tape while ensuring that the paper's part with ink is not in direct contact with the leather's surface.
- Using a pen, trace the drawing onto the leather and then take out the paper when you are done with the tracing and allow it to air for about two hours.
- Using a swivel knife, carve out the drawn pattern about ¼ to ½ the thickness of the leather.
- A correctly done carving will not need you to go through the next stage.
- Set up the deepest part of the beveller into the groove area and the other part on the area to be pressed down. Every time you beat it with a hammer or wooden/rubber head mallet, lay the stamping done before by two-thirds of the tool's length. This technique will enable you to carry out tooling of fifty percent of the leather's thickness. Expect to spend an excessive amount of time here with several hours spent beveling, tracing, carving, and finishing.
A major method used in this age and time is aiming to produce an effect in which the background is flat, and the foreground experiences a raise. You can use a flat tool that accumulates the suitable dye and leaves the background several shades darker than the foreground, thereby creating a contrast. During this process, there is an overlapping to prevent the markings from been too individualistic. The extent to which there is overlapping is also a choice to be

made by the leatherworker concerning the amount of time given to achieving a near-perfect job, with the energy expended in beating hard continuously for a very long time.

Setting up a carving image on the leather can also be done by the continuous and repeated stamping of a particular image repeatedly or using a sharp object such as an awl to form a speckled design by poking the leather in a precise way or by removing the background.

Materials needed for carving

A wooden or rubber head mallet

Bevellers (pointy, medium and small)

A swivel knife

Backgrounders

A strop

A strong wooden board with a strong rubber base

Waterproof tracing paper

A ballpoint pen

Spoon

Dyes and paints

Leather cement

Vegetable-tanned leather

Directions

- Get the pattern that you want to carve onto the leather printed out or draw it. The design should be formatted in such a way that it will fit in nicely to the space on the leather.

- Get the tracing paper set up and attach the paper with the image to it. Hold the two pieces of paper securely in place with masking tape. Trace out the image directly to the waterproof paper.

- Get a damp sponge and rub it on the surface of the leather to soften it up. There is the probability that the leather will get dried and hard when you are carving; all you need to do is simply soften it up again by making use of the damp sponge.

- Place the waterproof paper with the image traced out on it over the leather. Hold it firmly in place with suitable objects.

- Using a stencil, copy the image on the waterproof paper onto the leather. You can apply some paints to make the stencil lines more pronounced if you didn't get a clear image of the leather.

- Use the swivel knife to cut out some parts of the image that you want to be pronounced.
- A bit of stamping can also be done around the design pattern to give contrast and texture.

Burnishing Leather

The number of ways you can get that charming and attractive look to the edges of your leather piece is infinite. Leatherworkers have developed individual styles that differ from the next person. You can leave the edges of your project just the way it is without any finishing touches, apply some sort of paint to get a matte look or make it glossy; whatever burnishing method you decide to go with is determined by several factors that will eventually have the desired effect on the finished project. With the vast array of styles, I will discuss the foundation style that, as a beginner, will guide you on how to go about burnishing leather and eventually developing your style.

Steps
Cutting of the Leather
A properly measure cut is essential for well-adjusted alignment of your leather pieces when you join them. This is a basic leatherworking principle which you tend to overlook and try to boycott in your earlier days of leatherworking. You tend to see it as a relatively straightforward process that merely cuts of leather, joining them, and viola you are done with the project. The cutting process is one to which patience and unwavering attention are needed to ensure that you get the desired piece. To avoid the inevitable anguish that you will experience if your leather is not cut correctly, take your time to ensure that you don't rush through this stage.

Joining of the Leather
There is almost no action in leatherworking that is as simple as the joining of cut leather pieces. It sounds simple, and yes, it is simple. Since there are different joining methods, I will discuss a bit more about gluing here, and there are some factors that you need to consider with this method. Ensure you glue the piece as far as the edge to avoid it coming apart when you are burnishing. Making use of glue requires you to join one piece of leather at a time and not apply it to all the needed surface at the same time. This is because the glue dries quickly. Pick up one piece of leather and apply the glue to it before joining and moving onto the next piece. Always ensure that

you keep the glue application as straight as possible. A messy application can make some projects come out looking haphazard and unsightly. If such an accident should happen, you will have to take everything apart, and in the process, your leather will most likely suffer some damages. So you should take your time when applying the glue to avoid costly mistakes.

Another Cutting Process
After the gluing is done, go through the edges to confirm that they are all lined up well, and if by any chance there are some significant misalignments, gently cut that area off. If the misalignments are not that major, you can leave it as it will be taken care of during the sanding process.

Beveling
Most times, if stitching would be carried out along the edges, it is ideal that it should be done before you bevel. This is to bring about a curving finish to the edges, and this is a prerequisite to the sanding stage. The beveling is done to prevent the edges from curving in when you start to burnish.

Sanding
Sanding of the edges is a personal process that can be carried out with various grits depending on how you go about it. Some folks might use two grits, and others might go for more. Always sand for a short area at any given time to make sure that your hands remain flat during the process. I usually begin the sanding with one hundred and fifty grit sandpaper to bring out the area's elegant shape. This sanding gives a more finessed look to the relatively sharp and pointed edges resulting from the beveling. With this grit size, you should the leathers joined at that area should be reduced to the same level before you round it. You should also focus on getting rid of any excess glue that might be remaining in the area. The glue can be easily observed when sanding is it brings about a discoloration of the area. Sand continuous until every trace of the glue is removed because if there is any glue remained and you applied a dye, it won't accept the dye bringing about a patchy look in the appearance of that spot.

When done with the one hundred and fifty grit, move onto the six hundred grit to further smoothen the edges before finally finishing it off with an eight hundred grit size.

The Dyeing Stage

When dyeing the edges of the leather piece, extra care should be taken not to touch the main part of the piece, which most times would have already undergone some form of dyeing. You can get around this problem by constructing a makeshift paintbrush from pieces of wool or sponge that will get the job done.

Burnishing with a Wooden Slicker

With constant practice over some time, you will get the hang of this process. First, apply some tragacanth to a small area of the edge, arrange the area on the inner part of the burnisher in such a way that the notch picked in no way crimps the leather. Move the burnisher very fast in a to and fro motion along the edge in a firm yet gentle manner. The burnishing's primary purpose is to bring about the formation of heat by the friction been generated between the contact of the burnisher and the edge of the leather. This should continue until you hear a distinct sound. This is a signal that the burnishing is complete, and a visual cue is the shiny appearance of the edge.

Beeswax Application

This is done to make the edge appear warm and attractive with a soft glow. Apply some beeswax to the edges and rub it down with a piece of a soft cloth.

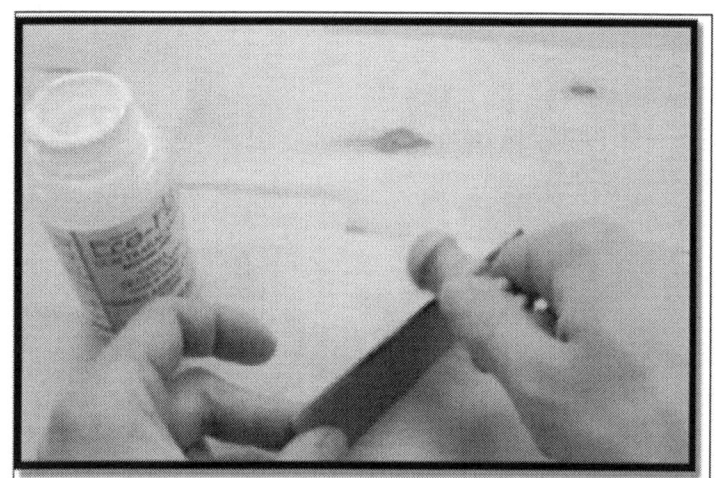

Chapter Four
Hole Punching in Leather

This section is dedicated to guiding you on how to punch holes in projects that require a hole and the best type of tools to make use in every situation.

Round Hole Drive Punch

The drive punch is the simplest, sturdiest, most-commonly used variety of leather hole punch. It comes in different sizes. The 3/32 inch leather punch makes holes for small jacket snaps and small rivets, the 1/8 inch drive punch makes holes for intermediate big rivets, and the 5/32 inch punch makes holes for significant jacket snaps. These dimensions can also be used to drill buckle holes and make holes for eyelets and grommets, but the density of the buckle pin or circumference of grommet or eyelet dictates the choice size of the hole punch.

There are cost-effective and diverse forms of hole punches. It works best for anyone who is confused about the type of hole punch to get or who doesn't make too many holes but needs to make multiple holes for the project at hand. Various sizes of extractable hole tube tips can be fixed to the body of the adjustable hole punch to suit the gap you want to make. The setback of this punch is that switching the ends is time-consuming.

Operational instructions for a drive punch

Begin with a robust and steady surface when you are drilling holes. Let's illustrate with a reliable tree trump. Set a piece of scrap leather or poly cutting board on the stump; this hinders the cutting edge of the drive from getting blunt or the punch from chewing the wood and destroying the cutting surface.

Tick the spots where you want the holes on leather with a pencil. Lay the leather on the stump and align the punch. Ensure that the hole punch is transverse to the leather. Maintain this position firmly, and hammer directly downwards according to the leather's density, the blow should puncture neatly with one or two strikes.

It is advisable to punch holes on a tree stump covered with leather to shield the drive punch. Different types of metals can be used, large poly head mallet, heavy rawhide mallet, or a simple carpenter's hammer. Using a metal hammer can expand the end of the punch as time goes on.

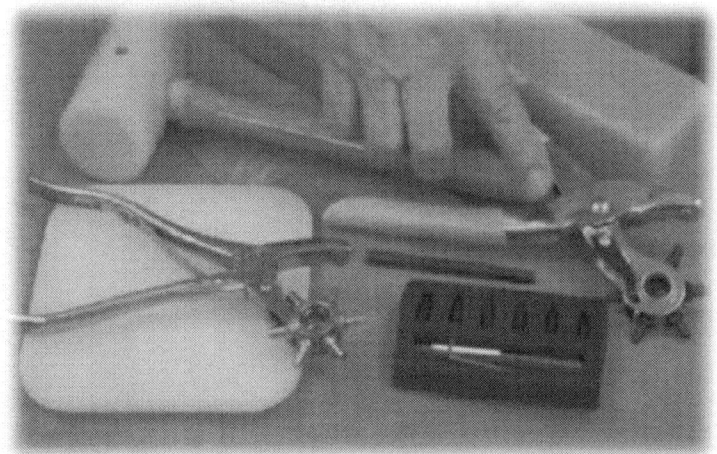

Economy Revolving Punch

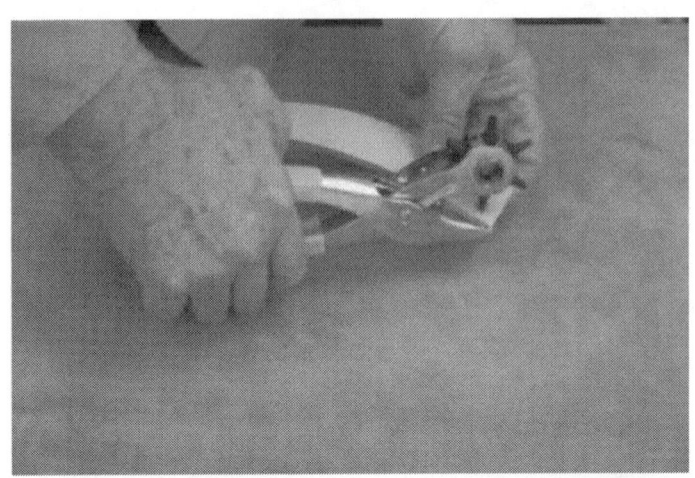

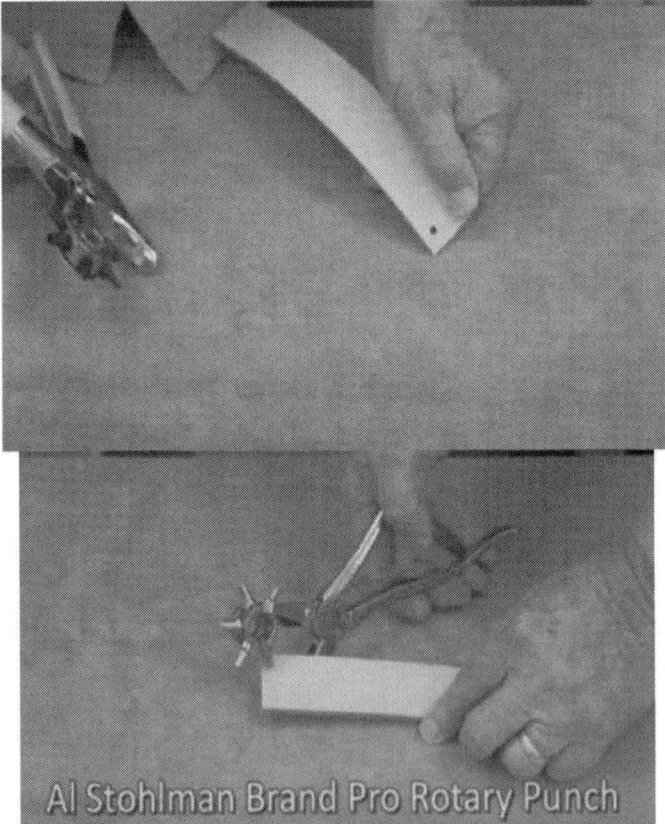

Al Stohlman Brand Pro Rotary Punch

Drive Punches

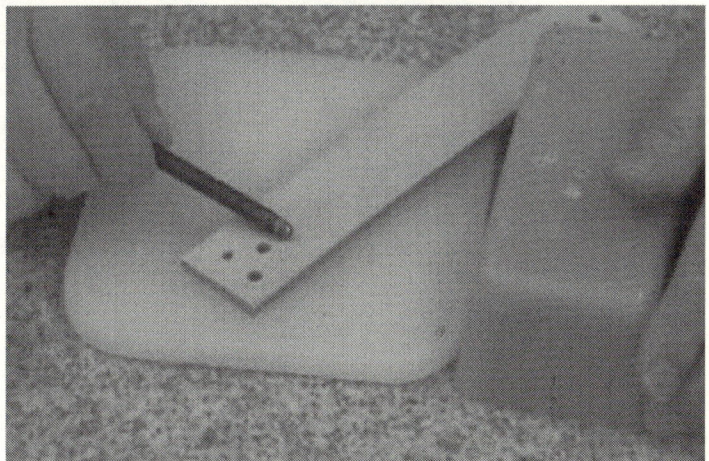

Creating a Buckle using an Oblong Punch for Leather

Oblong hole punch makes pin holes for belt buckles. It may need one or two more blows than a smaller drive punch. To make a hole on a rigid point, incline the oblong leather punch a bit to concentrate the strength of the hammer at that point.

You can substitute a round hole punch for an oblong hole punch if you cannot afford the price of an oval punch. Make two round holes with a distance of one inch between them; connect the round holes with two parallel cuts. You can make the parallel cuts with a knife or wood chisel. It is guaranteed that you wouldn't want to improvise ever again if you get your hands on an oblong punch.

The size of the buckle hole determines the type of oblong punch that you will use. If you can't bear the expense of various oval hole punch sizes, you can utilize the one you have. Punch a hole and then superimpose the blow on the previously made hole, projecting it beyond the said hole to the preferred length. Strike it with the hammer so that both borings create a prolonged hole. Use a poly cutting board beneath to shield the bench and the tool's cutting edge.

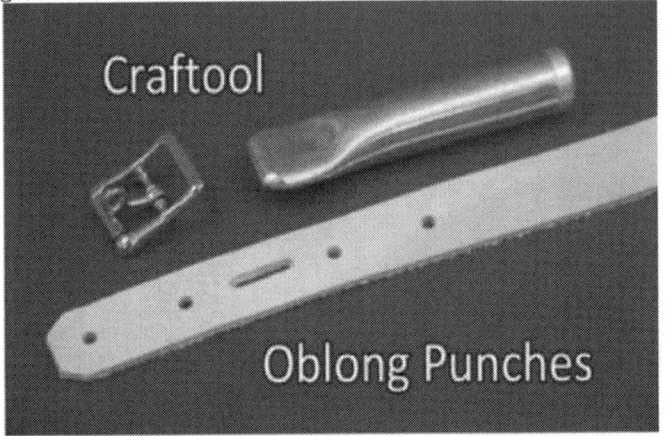

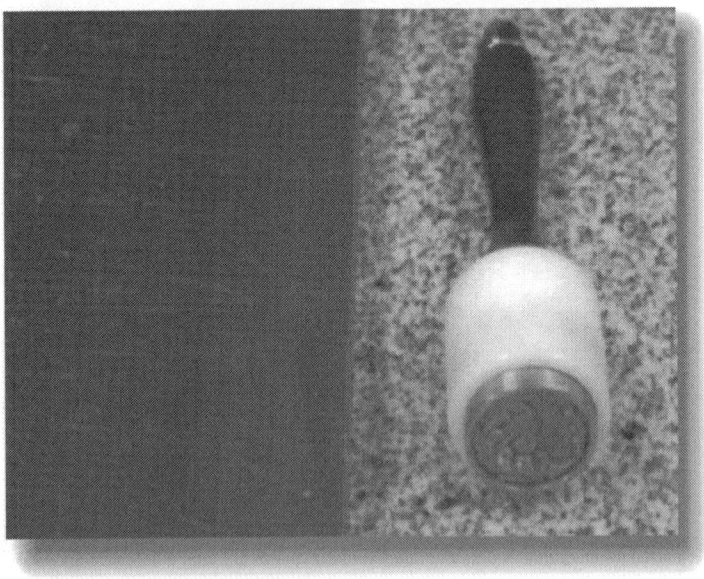

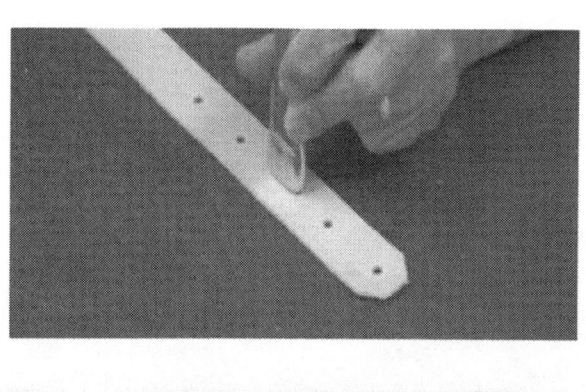

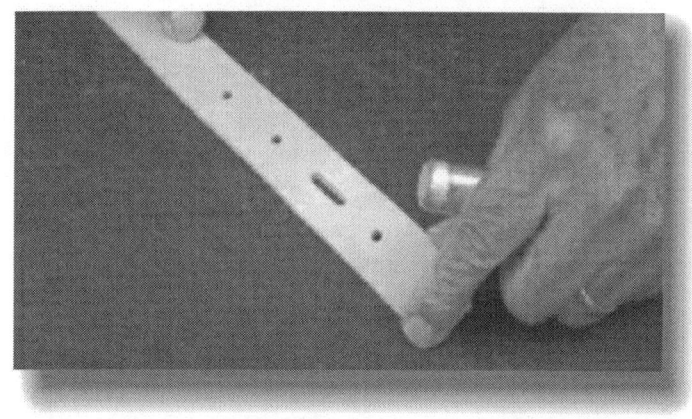

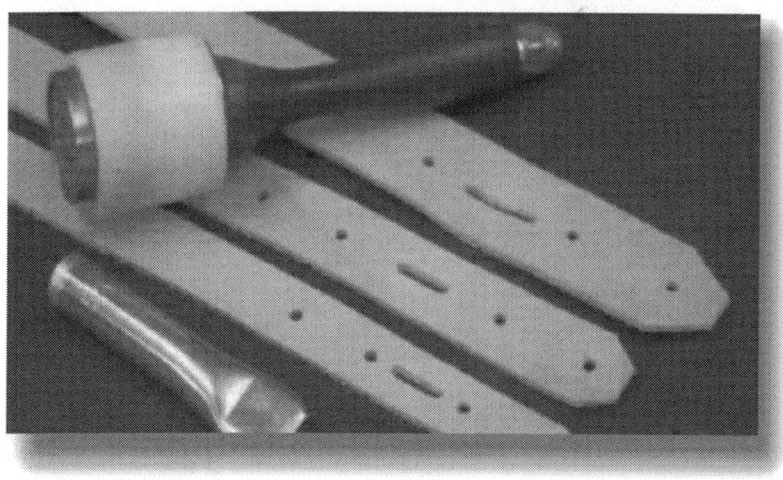

Making Circular Holes using a Rotary Punch

This device is fitting for drilling peculiar quick holes. The benefit of using the rotary punch is the ease of usage. It has six varying dimensions of punches that can be interchanged by spinning the wheel. This tool used to make an appearance at craft shows to drill extra holes on a belt when anyone asks for it.

The drawback of using the rotary punch pliers is that it exhausts the arms' muscles if you have several holes to bore. You also cannot use it to drill a hole in the middle of the material because it leaves a space of one inch away from the margin of the leather. The thickness of the leather is directly proportional to the size of the tube; it is difficult to force thick leather into a revolving punch. It is imperative to twirl the punch a bit to accommodate the leather jacket in cases like these. This leather device is excellent for odd punching holes, but it is stressful and challenging to drill several holes.

We cannot overemphasize the use of junk pieces of leather beneath the material you intended for drilling to protect the tool's edge. Without doing this, you are grinding the sharp blades of the tube unto the rugged metal anvil. The grinding will numb the pipe faster and weaken the metal anvil.

Drilling Round Holes for Lacing

A four-hole punch is mainly designed for lacing. Apart from the rotary punches and primary drive, there are special made leather punches for specific uses. An example of convenient tools in leather artistry is the four-hole punch; this tool is primarily for producing little holes for lacing leather. The individual hole on this punch has a 3/32 inch diameter, and a distance of ¼ inch separates them. The leverage of the four-hole punch over other types of punch is that it guarantees a uniformly spaced hole, and it is time-saving. This four-in-one punch is the best option to achieve a straight lacing hole, but the aforementioned single hole punch is more suited to creating curvy lacing holes.

The usage guideline of this hole punch is similar to that of the individual drive punch. As in the case of an oblong punch, it is also necessary to twirl the punch to concentrate the hammer's strength on a particular hole.

Dyeing

To confer color on the leather, you can either dye it or apply pigment to the exterior. Sometimes, leathers are dyed to get an even surface before treating with pigment finishes. Often, aniline dyes are used to bestow color intensity and improve the leather's organic grain feel. The most commonly used techniques of dyeing are:

- Brush dyeing
- Drum dyeing
- Spraying

The essential techniques for dyeing different leather are spraying and drum dyeing in the drumming procedure; skins are rolled in rotating drums holding the dye compounds, with allowance to maintain appropriate temperatures. The acid or basic dyes selection is influenced by preferred color, coloring methods, and successive culminating procedures.

In the spray technique, dyes in an atomized state are introduced to the leather with pressure spray guns, spraying booths, or automated sprayers. Spraying imparts extra color manifested in insoluble pigments that are afloat in water. Binding agents like shellac or casein can be mixed with pigment compounds; pigment coatings help the tanner ensure consistency and intensity.

Brush dyeing is employed in dyeing weighty leathers like tapestry hides strap sides and different unique leathers. The exterior of appropriately primed leather is grazed by a thin dye mixture a couple of times for color uniformity. When color is wanted on the surface of glove leather, the same method is used.

The Leather Dye Color Uniformity

Leather artists do not joke with color regularity; they usually look out for colors that give a uniform, natural finish to the leather. Color uniformity is primarily influenced by its speed of permeation while leather dyeing is ongoing; the rate of color penetration is inversely proportional to the color uniformity.

The Rub Off of Colors

Leather artists also pay close attention to the degree of color linkage with the leathers. The weak interconnection between the dye compound elements and the leather fibers is majorly responsible for color rub off. Color rub off is a massive problem because colors on bags or leather items used regularly can leave color residue on clothes or any other thing they touch. The correct choice of leather dye and subsequent use of unique fixing products can curb color rub off.

The Leather Dye Drying Time

Drying time is essential to everyone who crafts leather products. This is because drying time affects the production time and the quality of the finished product. Fast-drying causes a prominent color rub off. You have to search for a leather dye that creates a balance between the duration of drying and finished products.

The Leather Dye Application Sample

Consideration should be given to user convenience when picking leather dye. The leather dyes are usually applied by hand by the artist, but spray application follows the hand painting on a large scale leather production. You are required to gain mastery of how to create colored leather from natural leather with uniformly distributed dye to give a natural finish.

The Even Coating

Color regularity is usually desirable when producing colored leather, eliminating all forms of contrast in colors and shades. The exception to this is the creation of a vintage appearance on the finished product. Even if the dye is coated on the leather numerous times on the same spot, it must retain a near-even look. On rare occasions, a leather dye thinner comes in handy to reduce color intensity on the leather surface.

The Leather Dye Smell

Another important aspect of leather artistry is the smell, though there are more important factors to consider. The scent of leather dye is derived from the particles dispersed in the air when a dye bottle is opened. Alcohol or solvent-based stains have a more noticeable smell because they are very volatile. The reverse is the case in water-based dyes.

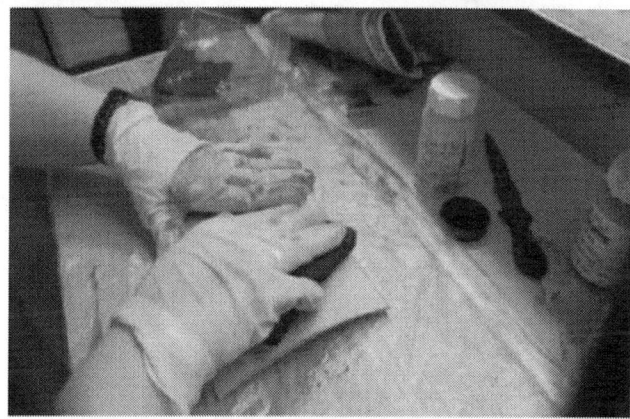

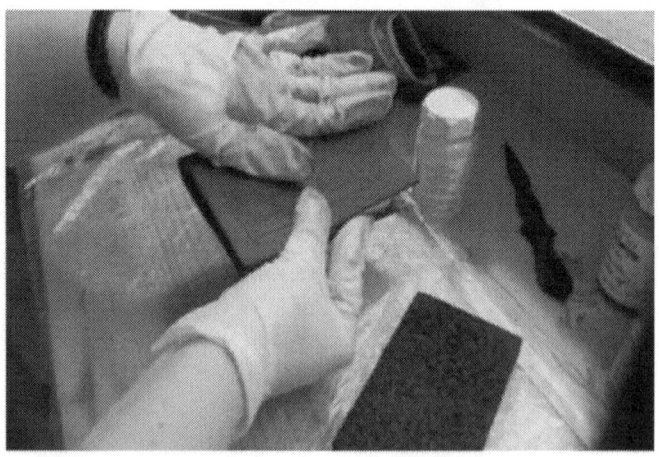

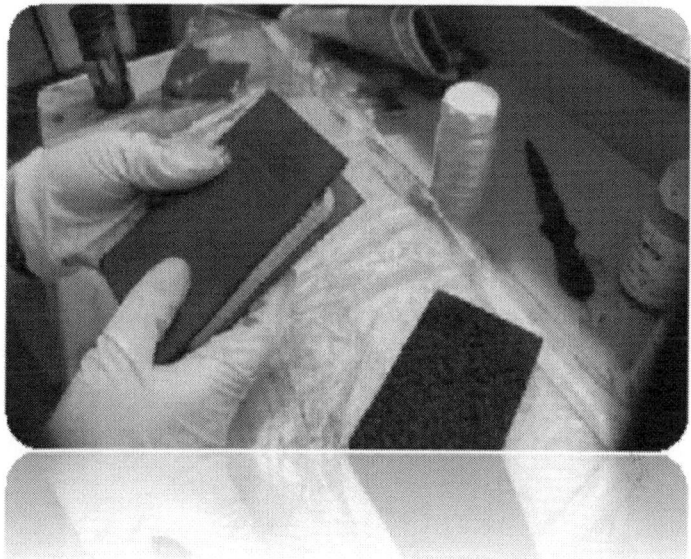

Procedures on administering leather finish

Leather finishes maintains the characteristics and look of the leather product. There are numerous things to note before application of leather finish:

- Every process must be completed before finish application
- Ensure that the surface area is moisture-less and utterly free of filth, dust or particles
- Apply the leather finish before you join and frame the product.
- Press a moist sponge lightly on the dye bottle; tilt it slightly so

that the dye runs onto the sponge.

- Apply a thin layer of finish to cover the leather's molded part, shifting the sponge circularly on the leather. Do this until the finish is imparted on the impressions and cuts.
- Allow the finish to completely dry. Cover the leather with another coat if you want a glossy finish, then let the leather dry thoroughly.

If you long for a sparkly finish, polish the leather with sheepskin or fluffy material. You can fix the different parts of the design together by lacing with leather or sewing with waxed thread.

Chapter Five
Stitching, Lacing, and Braiding
Procedures for Lacing

L acing bestows aesthetics appeal on hand-crafted leather items. The quality of lacing influences the appearance of the finished design. With the directions below and a routine exercise in lacing, you are on the path to becoming an expert in lacing.

Please, note that you should always lace with the completed part of the design directly opposite you.

Threading a 2-Prong Lacing Needle

You should stack the lacing needle with two yards of lacing at once. It is challenging to operate with more lengthy pieces of lacing; it weakens the lacing as it is dragged across the lacing holes.

The Process of Lacing and Connecting the Double-loop stitch

Suggestion: use 3/32 or 1/8 lace alongside slits or holes of the same dimension. The length of the lace in double loop lacing is about eight times longer than the design's actual length.

Sewing a Running Stitch

The length of lace required for this procedure is almost two times longer than the gap to be laced.

Procedures for lacing the Whipstitch: the methods for lacing whipstitch are employed on designs of regular starting and finishing ends like a billfold.

The lacing needed is about 3 ½ times the length to be laced.

Hand Stitching - Procedures for threading the needle

Fix a needle to individual ends of the thread according to the following guidelines.

Hand Stitching – Using Two Needles

For hand stitching, you need close to three times the length of leather you want to stitch.

Hand Stitching – Using One Needle

To hand stitch, you need close to three times the length of material you want to stitch.

Lacing Leather

Leather lacing bears a close semblance to the process of sewing fabrics. You need to drill holes in leather before lacing since it is a thicker and long-lasting material; this results in a broader distance than fabric sewing. As in sewing, several stitches can be employed in leather lacing.

Making Holes

A lacing chisel or a leather punch is the best tool in the formation of holes in your leather. Create quite, but not unreasonably wide holes to accommodate the lacing material. The material and the pattern you want to lace with will determine the width and size of holes.

Ensure that the distance between the holes are equal, with minimal space separating the holes from the leather's edge. Make holes on the two pieces you want to lace together and be attentive to the holes' alignment. It is possible to make the holes on both pieces at once with a punch if the leather is not too thick, which guarantees the precise alignment of the holes.

Stitching

A variety of stitches that produce diverse finished toughness and looks are available for selection when lacing. Running stitch is the most basic stitch. Harmonize the holes on both pieces of leather, and insert the lace, facing opposite directions, in the first holes. Insert the lace in the second holes, each end against its initial course, and replicate the process until all the holes are filled. Double running stitch enhances a running stitch without extra intricacies. When the running stitch is complete, repeat the procedure backwardly going the opposite direction.

A loop stitch can also lace leather. Run the lace through individual holes, turn the lace around to the first side and pass it through the next hole. The lace should pass through each hole in a similar pattern. This style offers a unique outlook than the running stitch. Attempt each of the stitches to decide which model works best for you.

Procedures for Sewing a Double Needle Stitch on Leather

- The double-needle stitch, also known as a saddler's stitch, tightly connects two pieces of leather. It is the tightest stitch in leatherwork.

- Ensure that the holes in both pieces of leather are uniformly aligned. Insert a waxed linen thread or synthetic sinew in a leather-stitching needle; do not fasten the thread end.
- Run the threaded needle through the first two parallel stitching holes from either direction. Pull the needle so that an even length of thread is on each side.
- Insert the free tip of the thread in another needle.
- Put the left needle to the right side of the next hole; put the right needle on the left side of the corresponding hole. Pull the two threads firmly. Replicate the procedure for subsequent holes.
- Towards the end of your stitching, take about three stitches rearwards. Continue with the original motion until you complete the stitching.

Procedures for Knitting with Leather

Knitted leather is pliable, rugged, and resourceful. Artists can knit anything ranging from bandana to tee shirt using a leather cord. Artists use light leather strips to make firmly twisted material and a dense strand for the loose weave. Flatten and weaken leather strips before the commencement of full knitting operation, use similar to a thick yarn.

Unpack the leather strips. Starting from the edge of strand, shape a few inches of the strand into a loop, and work the strand till it weakens. Go backward with the circle and work on the second side of the strip.

Replicate the procedure with the other portion of the strip. Go on with this motion until you have worked the full length of the strand. Flatten any strand that has been looped due to packaging by going with the curve. Weaken an especially difficult curved leather strip by stringing a bone bead on it. Tilt the dot so that it lightly scratches the leather, and then tug the bead down the strip.

Chapter Six

Sewing Leather on a Home Sewing Machine

Y ou will need:

Different needle sizes: tiny blades on the individual axis of the eye differentiate leather needles from traditional needles because leathers need small holes before threads can pass through.

Thread: nylon thread works best for leather because leather breaks down the standard cotton thread. It is not advisable to use polyester thread, for it cannot secure leather stitches. Choose a toneless thread.

Cutting leather: a sharp, elegant cut is compulsory for skillful leather. Use rotary blades or the most pointed scissors in your kit for thick leathers, and a knife for delicate leathers. It is important that you must not spare any expense in cutting leather if you want your designs to be always excellent.

Machine Setup

You need to modify some configurations on a household sewing machine. The leather needle makes a tiny hole in the leather with every stitch; elongate your stitch length to a minimum of 3.5 inches to avoid ripping or piercing the leather down the seam line.

You will figure out what tension level gives a lovely stitch by attempting to sow with different thread tensions. Ensure that you keep the beautiful side of the design up because of the leather's downside when sewing is always a bit irregular due to the puncturing before stitching.

Instruments

You need to have some equipment when designing with leather; a few may be available in the domestic kit.

Essential Necessities: knife, cutting soft leather with rotary blades will blunt the cutting edge rapidly; a utility knife will last longer.

A cheap cutting mat: a rotary cutting mat is not durable when working on it with a blade. Use a cheap and typical rotary mat that you are willing to discard.

Metal ruler: Get different sizes of metal rulers.

Adhesive: water-soluble cement is the best option for leather. You can also use standard contact cement as long as you strictly follow the safety guidelines.

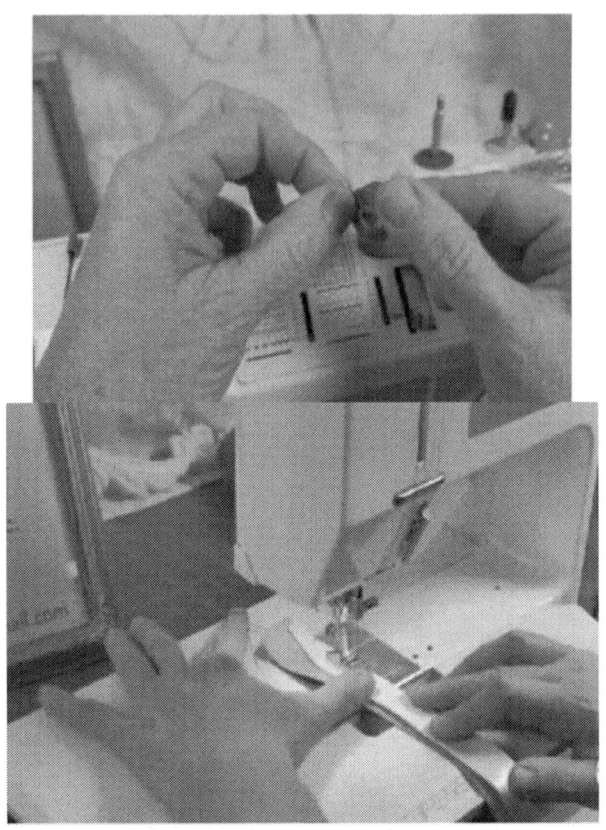

A mallet: a mallet is preferred to a hammer to strike leather equipment that cannot only damage the tools; it can cause you injuries as well.

Hole punches: rivets and snaps need the hole to be drilled in the leather at; first it is possible to use the two alternatively.

Lighter: it melts the tips of the thread to fasten them.

Optional Tools

Cobbler's hammer: this hammer flattens the thread of a seam. The advantage is that this hammer will not cast a mark on the leather from the margin due to its round surface.

Edge finish: gum tragacanth or beeswax works well as edge finish for designs.

Edge beveler: this gives an extra aesthetic appeal to the finish of the leather. It is similar in effect to sanding a chunk of wood.

This skill is a fitting hobby and an extra stream of income for most people with a zeal for sewing. Sewing leather and fabric are very different; leather usually has coarse exterior and robust formation because it originates from animal skin. For this reason, it is difficult to sew leather by hand.

A sewing machine effortlessly makes needle holes and stitch fast enough. Choose a sturdy needle for leather because they sometimes become fragile during leather stitching. Get all the tools you need for patterning, cutting, and making holes ready before you start sewing.

The use of different instruments, the required expertise, and leather sewing thickness make leather sewing more complicated than stitching and designing other materials. Comprehensive knowledge of how to use a domestic sewing machine to sew leather follows the simple procedures below.

- As always, the quality of a finished product largely depends on the quality of the raw material. Examine the leather for flaws and ensure it has even exterior. Choose from the different types of leather available - aniline, nubuck, pigmented, suede, faux, and semi-aniline. Take the longevity of the tools you will use on the leather into account.
- **Create a template as your yardstick**; This process enhances precision and saves time. This procedure is crucial because it provides a pattern to place, trace, and stitch your work. Reproduce the design on the new leather carefully without leaving a mark. Rotary cutter, Stanley or press knives, cardboard patterns, pen, and clicking press are tools that make tracing simple and easy.

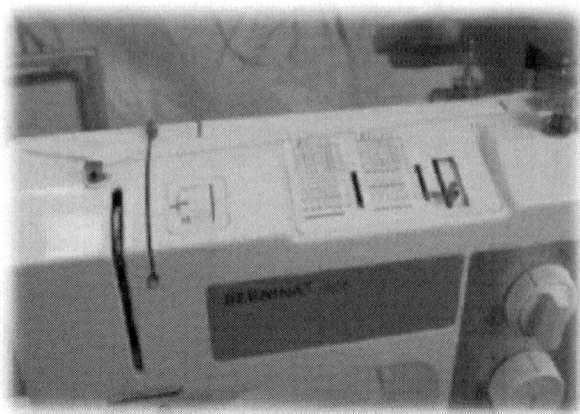

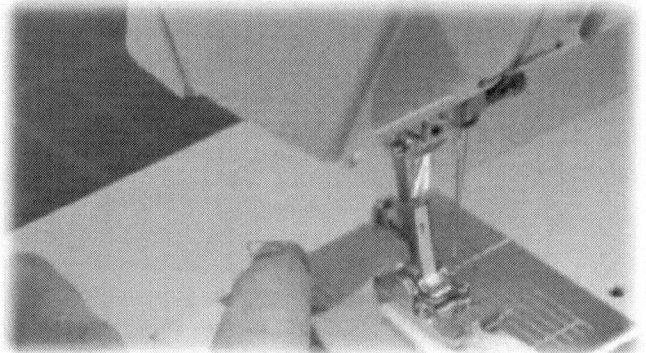

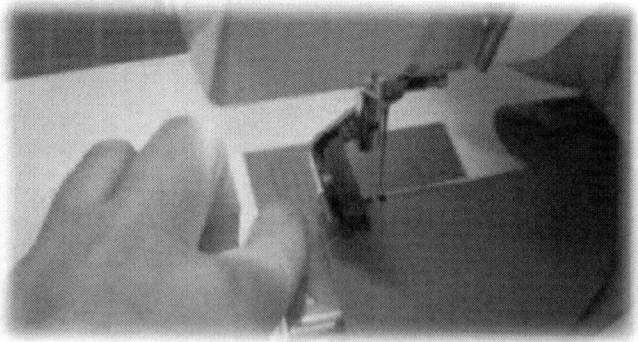

- **Press the leather to fit;** This procedure can come before or after the template creation. Press the leather till it's flat and is the right size to go beneath the presser foot smoothly; this ensures that the feed dog and needle can sew the leather without a hitch. Clipping the material or gluing them is a means to press leather for skillful sewing.

- **Use sewing machine needles dedicated to leathers;** Needles differ on account of their use and harmony with the sewing machine you own. Tiny needles are the correct ones for clothing materials, but a thick needle is the best for leather to facilitate easy penetration. Choose a long-lasting needle to prevent bending and interruption of the sewing process.
- **Pick the most appropriate sewing thread for leather;** It is essential to regard the leather thickness and longevity of the thread before sewing leather. Polyester or nylon thread is the best and frequently used for leather because they are sturdy and durable.
- **Fix an interfacing fabric;** This procedure is not mandatory since it depends on your material. An interfacing fabric secures your leather. This method usually conceals unwanted seams or marks on leather, consequently reducing flaws and making the project distinct. Please, note that you should use a thin cotton fabric in order not to make the leather heavier or appear so.
- **Ensure that the garment leather is flat;** This process prevents interference during stitching. You can achieve a flat leather by using thin interfacing cloth and applying adhesives thinly to the leather so that the leather will not expand. Maintaining a flat garment leather aids smooth running of the sewing machine and will protect the feed dog, needle, and presser foot.
- **Inspect the needle regularly;** Ensure that you inspect the needle after every stitch you run. The back and forth movement of the needle during leather stitching can make the needle edge-less, and it will call for a new needle. Keep as many spare needles as you can afford to save yourself stress if the present one you're using becomes weak and dull.
- **Smoothen the leather's surface with plastic equipment;** This process provides you with a parallel and light surface. Put the device beneath the presser foot but out of reach of the feed dog and needle. The essence of this procedure is to make the leather perpendicular to its surface to allow productive leather sewing. You can devise a tool as long as it serves the same purpose as a plastic tool.

- **Change the Presser Foot**; A presser foot that is consistently used adheres to leather and obstructs proper feeding of leather through the machine. The way to fix this is by merely switching the presser foot for a Teflon foot or roller foot, which works as best as presser foot.
- **Change the Stitch Length**; Use a stitch length that is longer than the usual you'd go for; a 3.5 is okay. You can prolong the stitch length as you want, but do not extend it beyond a basting stitch.
- **Tape but do not pin**; Do not use pins in leather because they will produce a permanent hole. Align the leather pieces and secure them with double-sided tape before sewing. Put a line of tape on both sides' margins, not going beyond the intended seam allowance. Then, sew. You can leave the tape on the leather; this is a norm in leather artistry. You would probably find a tape in the seam allowance of industrial leather products if you could manage a peek inside.
- **Always Assess Your Stitches First**; Leather stitches produce a lasting mark because of the slits the needles make in the leather. It is, therefore, not easy to correct errors in sewing as it is in fabric tailoring. Always use a junk piece of leather to test the tension, stitch length, thread, and overall running of your machine before starting the original work.
- **Plan efficiently**; A lot of domestic sewing machines cannot sew through thick and bulky leathers. Always choose basic designs that do not call for piling layers of leather on one another. The highest number of layers that can pass through a home machine without a hitch is three, including aspects required to sew along seams.

Sourcing Leather

You can get leather from several places. Working with a home machine demands getting thin leather. The standard measurement for leather thickness is in ounces, use 3oz or less on a home machine.

You can find leathers at a thrift store. Though the leathers don't always look catchy, no worries, it's not for dress up. You can make use of them to cut out parts.

Online stores for leather are everywhere. Proceed with caution because you do not know what will be delivered to you. Order small pieces or sample material to test and ascertain the quality.

Chapter Seven
Guidelines on Gluing Leather

G luing comes in handy in leather artistry, either to repair a piece of leather, attach pieces to sew effortlessly, or join two leather pieces into a completed design. It is, therefore, essential to learn how to do it properly.

Gluing leather goes smoothly with a neat workspace, appropriate tools, and the right adhesive. All you need to do is get the glue ready, apply it uniformly, roll or strike it with a hammer to hold it in place and dry it according to glue specification. Store the glue suitably so that it will be useful for subsequent projects.

Some straightforward but essential procedures ensure an effective gluing process. Let's consider and review the intricacies so that the project ends up beautiful.

Summary of Leather Gluing Procedures

Gluing leather is fusing two pieces of items with an even covering of adhesive. The vital aspects include picking the suitable equipment, glue, application technique, and right implementation. Once you understand your way around it, it's reasonably straightforward. Gluing leather is an excellent way to fuse finished products that should be pliable and sturdy.

What is Leather Glue?

Every type of glue is not suitable for leather. The majority of leather artists endeavor to utilize super glue or conventional adhesives on leather, but they can damage the leather in a snap of the fingers.

Pay keen attention to the parts of leather you want to join before choosing glues. Choose the appropriate adhesive for the material, and also can hold pieces together firmly. Be cautious about picking fitting glue; it should be impenetrable and durable.

There are different types of glue available in the market for leather. Pick the corresponding glue to fit the particular leather you need to join or fix. I'd nominate the rubber cement for leather as the best option. This glue is durable but can get grimy and slimy with usage. There are specific glues for specific purposes; glue for the leather bag is different for leather shoes.

Procedures for Gluing Leather

Most people are likely to choose glue in their surroundings to fix leather; the most common and frequently used is super glue, leather glue, or contact cement. Super glue is the most popular among domestic artists. More often than not, they get curious about whether super glue works on all leather products like shoes, wallets, or bags.

Though super glue is perceived to be multi-functional, it is not the most fitting glue for every leather product. It certainly doesn't measure up to expectations in finished leather items.

If you are inexperienced and use super glue for leather, you will most likely struggle or ruin it. Therefore, it is crucial to choose the correct paste based on what you intend to rectify. You must seek a strong adhesive, but you must also consider the material you plan to use it on before choosing glue for leather craft. Without paying attention to the material, even the best glue might not yield the expected result.

The techniques of repairing vary according to the products you want to mend. Let's explore the procedures involved in gluing leather extensively.

Identification of the material
Before choosing and applying glue on leather, mentally decide on the material you intend to join with leather. It might be leather to wood, leather to leather, or leather to any kind of material. So, deliberate ahead of time and duly prepare.

Needed materials:
Paper napkin, leather material, fitting leather adhesive, clamps

Leather Gluing for Sewing versus Joining Material
You can glue leather for various reasons. Occasionally, it is to create a momentary bond to assess the appropriate point where pieces come together. Mild glue with moderate adhesion that is easy to remove work best in this scenario. For example, the usual Elmer's or PVA glue.

If you want to sew materials, glue helps align and secure the edges of the material while stitching through with a machine. Here, the glue that will stay in place beneath the material is not too strong at the same time.

When you intend to use glues as the primary medium to fuse leathers enduringly, contact cement always works well. It is pliable, water-resistant, reliable, and durable.

Guideline to Gluing Leathers in Ten Steps

1. Get the work surface ready

An extensive, smooth, and work free surface is the best for gluing. A table or a workbench will suffice, laying some papers on the surface to protect and maintain the surface's neatness from any glue that might drop. Provide enough space for equipment, movement, and other activities. Occasionally, the ability to move around the table without hindrance improves the gluing process; this is not a prerequisite, but it doesn't hurt to indulge. In as much as you have sufficient space to work, you are good to go.

2. Obtain the appropriate tools

Though leather glue requires just a few tools, they facilitate the expected result. Let's look into them and learn their mechanism of operation and usefulness.

Leather glue and adhesive

Various kinds of glues are on the market for leather. A few of them produce a momentary bond with a crude outcome that is readily removed and reapplied. Other adhesives are firmer, more forceful, and harder to remove. Some glues swell inside the materials during drying; still, some are indestructible. When the sturdier adhesives are used, an attempt at separating the attached pieces will probably ruin the leather.

Leather glue pot

Glue is a valuable addition to your running leather gear; the common challenge is that they dry if it remains open when you are working. A glue pot is a little plastic, an air-tight container that holds glue and adhesives. Glues can stay for a while in a glue pot without drying up.

To use the glue, loosen an air-proof cover to expose a brush and a fraction of the adhesive. Immerse the brush into the glue and use it on the leather. When you are through, replace the air-proof cover by fastening it, and the adhesive will retain its properties until the subsequent uses. Gluepot comes in handy to preserve glues if you carry out a lot of gluing.

The glue spreaders

Glue spreaders are usually tools with smooth margins and come in plastics. They ensure uniform distribution of glues on even surfaces, permitting the light spread of adhesives or glue concentration on a certain point. After use, clean, and use again. Retaining the flat borders is crucial to even distribution of the glue.

Glue application brushes are not necessities in dispersing glue, dip in a liquid glue and use on the leather. They accelerate the application of large amounts of glue, although glue spreaders do a more fantastic job of even spread. In summary, spreaders simply aid glue dispersion and concentration.

Hand leather rougher

A rough surface improves the strength of the bond between materials. When the intended materials to be joined are smooth, a hand leather rougher scrapes the surface and produces the needed rough layer. This created rough layer will catalyze the fusion of the materials. Hand rougher are the norm in saddle making and related work.

Leather edge clamp

Leather clamps are unique instruments built with steel but the clamp jaws with rubber. The jaws are very even so that they do not mar the leather; the rubber covering on the clamp jaw ensures that it is almost impossible to leave marks. Furthermore, the rubber aids the clamp to hold the leather firmly. Some other varieties of edge clamps are made of metal, while some clamp jaws are coated with leather to accomplish the same purpose rubber will.

Edge clamps also grip the attached leather pieces in place during the drying of the glue. It is also essential in cases where an instrument works best to secure a part of the material than ordinary hand will. It also helps to smoothen and spread out leather.

Leather weights
Leather weights are little metal tools that keep leather steady during punching, stamping, gluing, or cutting. They also flatten the leather further into a smoother working surface. They have even glossy surfaces so that they will not leave a mark on the leather when they are on top. They are usually made of steel or brass.

Leather often moves during cutting or shifting. It is also possible to have an unwanted but standard curve in thick leathers during cutting; leather weight will fix these problems by holding leathers in place or keeping the leather flat to avoid bends. Leather weights are available in different sizes.

Though there are specialized leather weights, you can use anything as a leather weight as long as their exterior will not scrape or wound the leather.

Leatherworking shoe hammer
Leatherworking shoe hammers are usually utilized for ensuring striking stitches, holding attached leather pieces in place, tapping through sharp folds. They possess a large, dense steelhead that creates a profound, stable effect. They are common in bag, saddle, and luggage making, and shoemaking as well.

Leatherworking metal roller
Leatherworking metal roller flattens joined leather layers. A precise tool for this purpose is beneficial because leather can sometimes be thick and also common has a beautifully completed even surface. Removal of air gaps and bubbles contribute to the beautiful outcome and fantastic appearance of the leather.

The metal roller consists of a solid, dense metal cylinder joined to a handle. When tugged at, the roller rolls across the leather, putting pressure and ensuring that a firm fusion is created between the leather surfaces.

Rags
Rags serve the purpose of wiping up glues and occasionally to press it down and flatten it. Lint-free cloths like used cotton blouses or microfiber fabrics

will fit the bill.

3. Prepare the leather surface

Rough surfaces produce superior adhesion because uneven surfaces give more space for the glue to stick. It is beneficial to roughen the surface to reveal the slam leather fibers during gluing; this increases the effectiveness of glue and contact cement with leather.

You might need to leave the leather surface even if the joined pieces are sewn or desire a highly tight tolerance between the materials. Nonetheless, it is advisable to always roughen the leather with a hand leather rougher or wire brush.

Leather surfaces should always be clean and free of dirt; brush some deglazer lightly on unfinished leather to remove the dirt and residues on it. For a milder method, a lint-free cloth removes thin dirt and fragment on completed and fragile leather.

You can proceed with gluing when the surface is clean and ready.

4. Prepare the glue

Glue sometimes can be thick and stiff; they are usually thinned to become lighter and more free-flowing and dry with minimal bulk. Even with this, they still maintain their potency. There are different thinners made, especially for glues and contact cement.

Manufacturers usually sell thinners that works best for their glues, according to corresponding constituents. The common unspoken rule for thinning contact cement is mix 2/3 cement with 1/3 thinner, though different manufacturers may give another prescription. So, you should read the instructions that accompany the products to keep you on track.

You can either use your glue directly from the tube or a glue pot if you like its original consistency. Glue pots are a great way to preserve thinned glue from drying out. Store large portions of glue in a glass container; it yields more amazing results than plastic. This will save you the stress of preparing glue for coming projects.

Once you have prepared your glue, it is ready for usage.

5. Use the adhesive/glue

Gluing is the most exciting aspect, and it is quite straightforward. Begin with applying the glue in the middle of the item to disperse across the rest of the material, though most of the adhesive will remain in the middle. The strong glue is then spread uniformly across the surface. Starting the gluing procedure from the center promises the best, and most effortless result, beginning at the edges, makes the distribution difficult, and may even mess up the leather's edges or the work surface.

Use a leather glue spreader or glue brushes (paintbrushes, in some cases, or specialty brushes packed with the glue) to distribute and thin out the glue from the center of the material. Ensure that the glue is dispersed uniformly and smoothly across only one surface. However, both surfaces should be smeared with glue when the choice is contact cement. The coming step is mandatory if you are utilizing contact cement.

6. Allow the contact cement to dry

The glue needs to dry for about twenty minutes when using contact cement before joining the materials. Remember that both surfaces have been smeared with the adhesive. While they are drying, they will get a bit sticky. Then, you can join the surfaces together.

A little trick for when you are designing with thick leather, or one that has a coarse or spongy surface and you desire excellent bonding strength, consider applying a layer of contact cement, and then dry for about twenty minutes. Proceed to spread a second coat of contact cement on both surfaces. The first coat of contact cement will stick to the leather, filling a few pores in the surface; then, the second covering will give a more uniform and smoother layer of contact cement for the other surface to bond.

A running fan or hairdryer will accelerate the drying process, and consequently, save time.

7. Press the layers together

After the contact cement or glue application, and the contact cement is a bit sticky, proceed to merge the pieces of leather. Give your best to make the bond smooth, firm, and uniform for professional and breathtakingly beautiful outlooks. A few instruments can help you to achieve this.

Start by placing the leather together and ensure that the edges are aligned to your satisfaction, then press with your hands. Some tools can accomplish this. A leather roller will press flat pieces to produce standard and regular outcomes. A hammer with a broad head helps to strike the leather together, place scrap leather pieces between the hammer and leather to avoid marring of the project by the hammer. The hammer also plays a vital role in the gluing of tight, bent, or far corners. Both leather rollers and hammer expels surplus air and glue.

8. Hold the leather firmly during drying
Holding the leather in place is essential after gluing and flattening out; this will keep the surfaces steady, unmoving during drying, assuring a strong bond. Several tools can facilitate this. The leather clamp is an example; it holds the pieces tightly clamped together while drying. Placing leather weights on the glued leather pieces keep them in place for drying. Anything rugged and that won't leave a mark will serve the purpose of securing leather pieces during drying. You can keep between your leather weight and glued leather pieces.

Another tool that functions in this regard is a vise; they have teeth in the clutches with leather in-between them. The attached leather pieces can shield the leather in the grips. You have to be cautious with a vise because too much pressure can mark or ruin the attached leather's shape or cause any artist nightmare: move the leather out of place.

9. Clean up surplus glue
You've done a great job of setting the leather; now, it's time to wipe off residual glue from edges and surfaces before it dries completely. You can use a lint-free cloth, or a moist rag if the glue is already tacky. An eraser will do the job in some cases as long as you are patient and careful not to mar or ruin the leather beneath it.

If you do not have an air-proof container for keeping brushes, wash them thoroughly and dry. Make sure that there is no glue to join any brush to a glue pot if you used one; before fastening the lid of the glue pot, ensure that there is no adhesive around the edge of the pot or the cap. This will guarantee that the pot can be unscrewed later.

Maintain an upside-down position when keeping adhesives in pots, cans, or tubes, especially those with in-built brushes. This technique ensures that the items in the container are close to the /top of the container and prevents drying at the points where they are fastened. It will also keep them handy and useful. With the upside-down position, put in a plastic bag and tape to prevent leakage unto the tabletop or rack.

There should be enough glue in the container to cover the tip or the brush to prevent drying. When you realize how priceless functional adhesives are, you'd want to keep them for as long as possible. Store thinned glues in small glass jars or canning to maintain the moisture and consistency of the adhesive.

10. Allow the adhesive to dry
You have finished the most challenging aspect of the job. Grab a seat, sit comfortably, and let the glue work its magic. Drying can take place from a few hours for some adhesive to 21-48 hours for bulkier adhesives and contact cement. Exercise patience, and you will have a beautifully connected leather piece

Procedures for Gluing Leather to Metal

Joining leather to metal is complicated because of the differences in the physical properties of the materials. Fortunately, we have a couple of adhesives that can accomplish the task. Unique superglue-style adhesives have sufficient adhesive strength to join the surfaces, cement and shellacs are more appropriate for fragile projects because they have less adhesive strength. Your leather to metal fusion will be effortless with a suitable adhesive.

- Choose the correct glue for your project; you have two fundamental alternatives. You can either use a superglue-style product or household goop if you want an enduring, strong adhesion. Both products are excellent on metal or leather surfaces, coarse or with grime. Use cement glue if you want to detach the surfaces after a while or attach importance to aesthetic value. Rubber cement attaches the metal to leather and is water-soluble. Shellac-based glue gives a firm fusion that can be dissolved with an alcohol solution.
- Scour the metal surface with sandpaper or steel wool. This will remove or prevent rust and result in a better surface for the glue to stick.
- Use the preferred adhesive on the leather and metal surface.
- Align, join, and secure both surfaces in place. Do this instantly if you chose a rapidly drying adhesive to prevent the glue from drying.
- Keep both surfaces steady until a firm adhesion is created.

Superglue and rubber cement will create the bond rapidly. Shellac glue requires close to 72 hours of drying to complete the bonding.

Guidelines for Gluing Leather to Wood

It is also possible to mend leather furniture. Pick glue that ensures the most reliable and most durable bond because wood and leather are contrasting materials. The cement contact is the best and most productive glue when attaching the leather to wooden furniture. Scrape the fleshy side of the leather with sandpaper beforehand, then spread contact cement on it with glue applicator or foam brush. Then, allow it a moment to dry until it is glutinous.

Smear the second coat of contact cement on the leather after the first layer has become glutinous, and then allow the second coat to become glutinous. Position the leather on the wood and push down firmly to enable the items are wholly joined to the wood.
Use a hammer to exert force on the attached aspect. Leave the piece till the glue does its job entirely.

Guidelines on Gluing Fabric to Leather

To join fabric to leather, you have to learn the method of attaching leather and fabric surfaces in a manner that forms firm adhesion while maintaining the flexibility of both materials. There are two kinds of glues that serve this purpose; spray-on glue forms a weak adhesion but dries clear, while contact glue forms a very sturdy bond.

- Clean the surfaces with a dry rag; dampen the cloth with water and drag over both surfaces to remove tacky residue. Air-dry the two surfaces.
- Apply the glue. For contact glue, smear a mild layer of glue on the leather and fabric. In the case of spray-on adhesive, keep the spray can three inches away from the leather and spray a drizzle of resin on the leather. Replicate the process for the fabric.
- Place the surfaces with glue on each other, press together, and firmly hold it in place for about two minutes. Place a weighty item on the attached materials and leave for close to four hours, or as long as possible to guarantee a dry, sturdy adhesion.

Hints: Often, leather adhesives are pliable, but super glue and contact cement are the exceptions; you cannot alter the items after applying these glues. Therefore, ensure that you position the pieces correctly and be attentive after the attachment.

If you choose to hold the leather down with clamps, wind tissue paper around it. Else, the clamps can mar the leather for good.

Use a fair amount of glue if the gluing purpose is sewing because extravagant use of glue can impede sewing or produce a slit.

Don't ever touch the grain side of the leather with glue because it is not removable, and leaves a lasting mark. Pay attention to the leather side to apply glue because the grain side of the leather never sticks, irrespective of your glue choice. Always use glue on the flesh side.

Always wear gloves during gluing with contact cement, because it is challenging to expel contact cement from the skin.

N eeded materials:
   Pen
   Awl
Safety pin
Artificial sinew
Cord
Leather
Ruler
Shears
Rivets and rivet setter
Sewing punch
Stitching needle or sewing machine

Directions

- Settle on a particular size and measure it out on the leather. A 20-by-18 inch measurement will leave you with a medium-sized bag. Divide the material with sheers and spread in a manner such that the short end makes the upper and lower end of the leather. From the upper and lower part, measure 3 inches away from each side, and mark each point visibly with a pencil.

- Fold the leather equally so that the lower part is over the upper part. Measure and mark one inch from the new lower end, and punch holes at the left and right side of the marked distances with a punch. There will be four holes when you are done.

- Fix the human-made threading material through the stitching needle. Begin sewing the halves together from the 4-inch mark. Create a slit through the leather with an awl to ease the stitching. Sew the two edges together, ensuring that the holes at the 1-inch mark beneath remain aligned.

- From the leather overlapping each other above the stitches, fold the upper part down. Pull the edge down with just one inch and pin on both sides with supplementary stitching needles, sew the folding down from end to end. Turn the backpack and replicate the procedure for the second side.

- Flip the backpack inside out so that the stitches are now inside. Put a rivet in each of the 1-inch holes and secure them with a rivet setter.

- Cut two 2-yards strands of leather, pin one end with a safety pin. Pass the strand through the band above the backpack using the safety pin to navigate through the band. When the strand appears on the other end of the band, remove the pin, and replicate it for the second side. Insert each end of the strand in the rivet in its corresponding direction and fasten them to create straps.

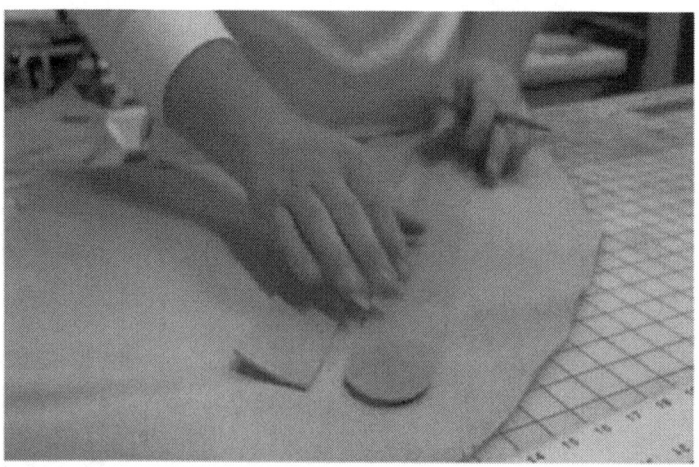

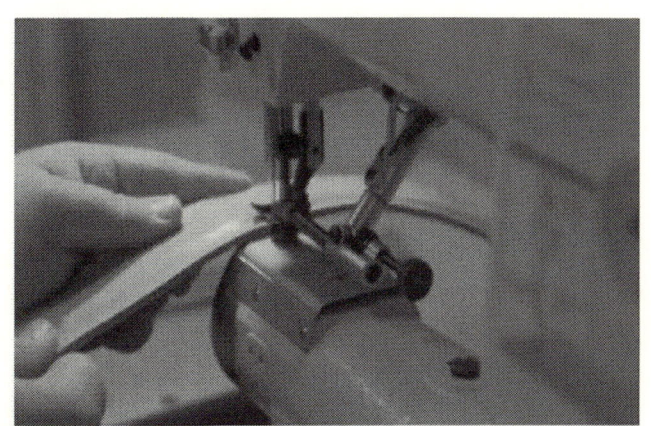

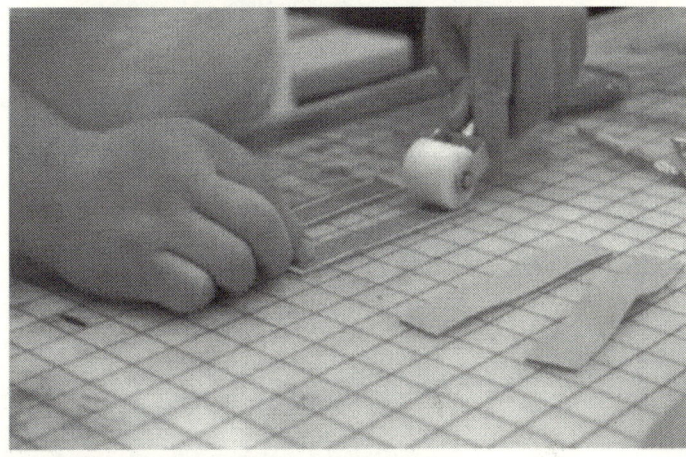

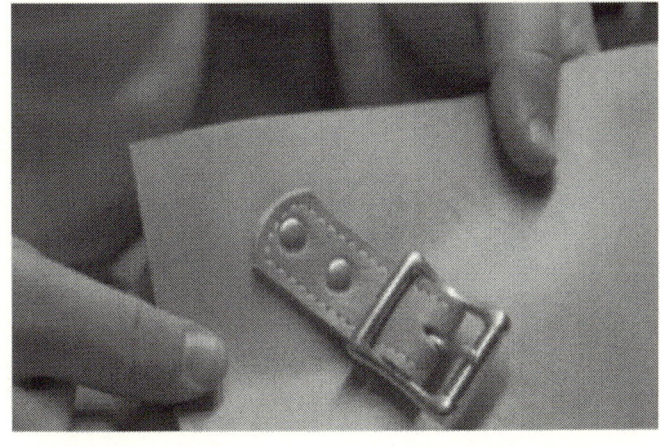

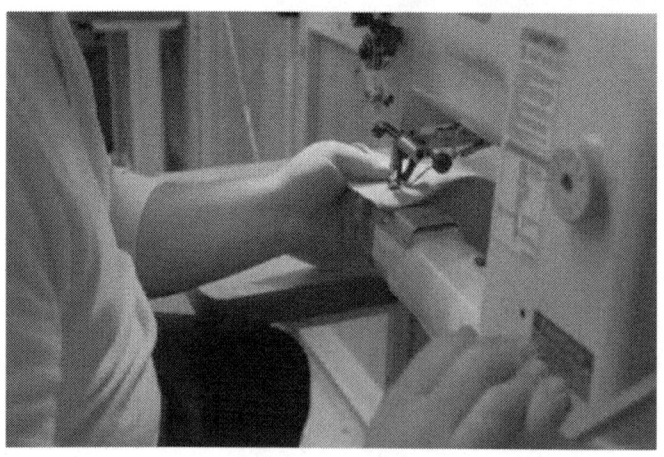

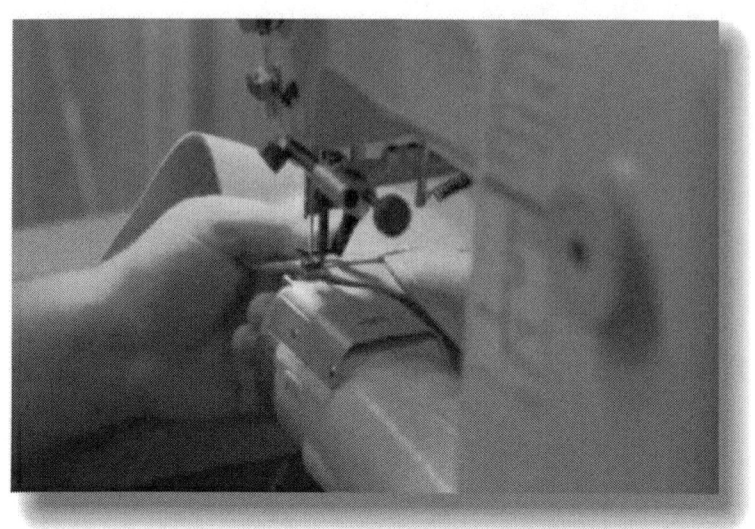

Leather Pouches for Children

Needed materials
One cut of 8-by-18 inch leather
Small pieces of different leather for precise and particular features
A leather needle
Awl
x-acto knife
Three 2-by-42 inch strands of fabric
Waxed linen cord
A cutting mat, sharp scissors

Directions
- Cut out shapes, features, or any other particulars you want to add to the top overlap. Trace the edge of a dish with a pen and cut the traced line with shears. Measure six inches away from the side and create a circular, triangular cut with the x-acto knife to form ear flaps. Use the negative gap to fix the straps.
- Position your shapes and special features on the open flap; punch holes on the layers of leather with the awl. Pull them apart, make

wider holes, and then stitch them to the front flap. In the case of felted wool or vinyl, a gorilla or fabric glue will be great to attach your shapes and other particulars.

- Braid your fabric strands to form a strap, stitch each end on the pouch interior so that the straps are poking out of the ear holes. Fold the side up, drill holes through the sides using the awl, stitch them up starting from the top to the base, and back up.
- You can alter this design into a pouch for item collection by adding a clasp and some facial features to give a creature semblance.
- You will need the following materials for the modification: one piece of 8-by-14 inch leather, small pieces of different leather or felt for precise and particular features, a leather needle, awl, x-acto knife, three 2-by-42 inch strands of fabric, waxed linen cord, a cutting mat, and sharp scissors.
- Cut a small strand of 1" x 3" of fabric, mark 1 inch away from the edge of the significant leather piece, and stitch the leather strand on the marked point. Do the stitching in a way that the strand is almost folded like a caterpillar. You should create slits beforehand with an awl and pass the waxed linen through the needle. Knot the strand behind the leather.
- Round off the other side with a dish; make a middle circular-cut 1.5 inch over the rounded edge. Make sure that your cut is more significant than the strand to fit through the cut.
- Overlap the pouch and stitch both ends. Cut tiny holes on the same point you fixed the ear flap in the old pouch, and insert the tips of the strap through the gap to the bag interior, and then stitch to hold down.
- Add two pieces to form the eyes and stitch.

Leather Cufflinks

Needed materials
Leather scraps
Scissors
Sticky glue
Alphabet punch
Gold cufflink

Directions

- Trace the borders of your gold cufflinks on leather, and cut out the shape. This process is the most challenging aspect of the design. Try as much as possible to make the circles as round and precise as possible. Make use of the flimsiest leather to ease this step.
- Moisten the leather circles with a damp tissue paper and punch in the letter. Attach to your cufflinks with glue and allow it to dry.

Hand-made passport cover

Needed Materials and tools
Contact cement
Leather
Beeswax
Waxed thread
Awl
Cutting mat
Two leather needle
Knife
Stitch spacer
Metal ruler

Directions
- This design requires sufficient leather for the original cover and two flaps on the inside. Cut a 7 inches x 5 inches cover and each fold

should be 2 ½ inches x 5 ½ inches.

- Place the pieces in their positions, mark the point where the flaps will be, separate the parts, and smear contact cement on the exterior margins.
- Allow the adhesive to dry totally before pressing the pieces together. Holding the pieces in place will ease the stitching.
- Position the flaps down on the workbench, put the ruler 1/8 inches away from each end, and run the stitch spacer through the edge. This procedure will evenly mark each stitch; exert a lot of force to get a lovely pattern.
- Press individual edge with the awl to get an imprint that extends far down for the needles to pass through. Then, insert the thread in the leather needle and start sewing. It is quite simple to thread a needle, insert the thread in the eye, pull the tip down totally along the eye, and fasten the thread's end. To further tighten the thread, wax the thread with some beeswax.
- Finish up the stitching in a crossing pattern across the leather; individual needle passing through the consistent hole, be cautious to avoid stitching through the thread.
- During sewing, tug at the stitches firmly to maintain a neat outlook. It is not advisable to get a vice or saddle for only a project; it is the most appropriate tool for sewing. Lacing saddle is a necessity if you will be hand stitching for more leather projects.
- Hand sewing takes time, but be patient through the process to ensure that you have neat and firm stitches backstitch through three holes after sewing all the edges to tighten the thread, and then cautiously cut the tips. Even out the stitch with overstitch wheel to push the thread down the leather and tidy the stitches outlook.
- Round the corners using scissors or knife, wax the edges, and smoothen with your fingers. Your passport is ready, book that flight, and tour the world!

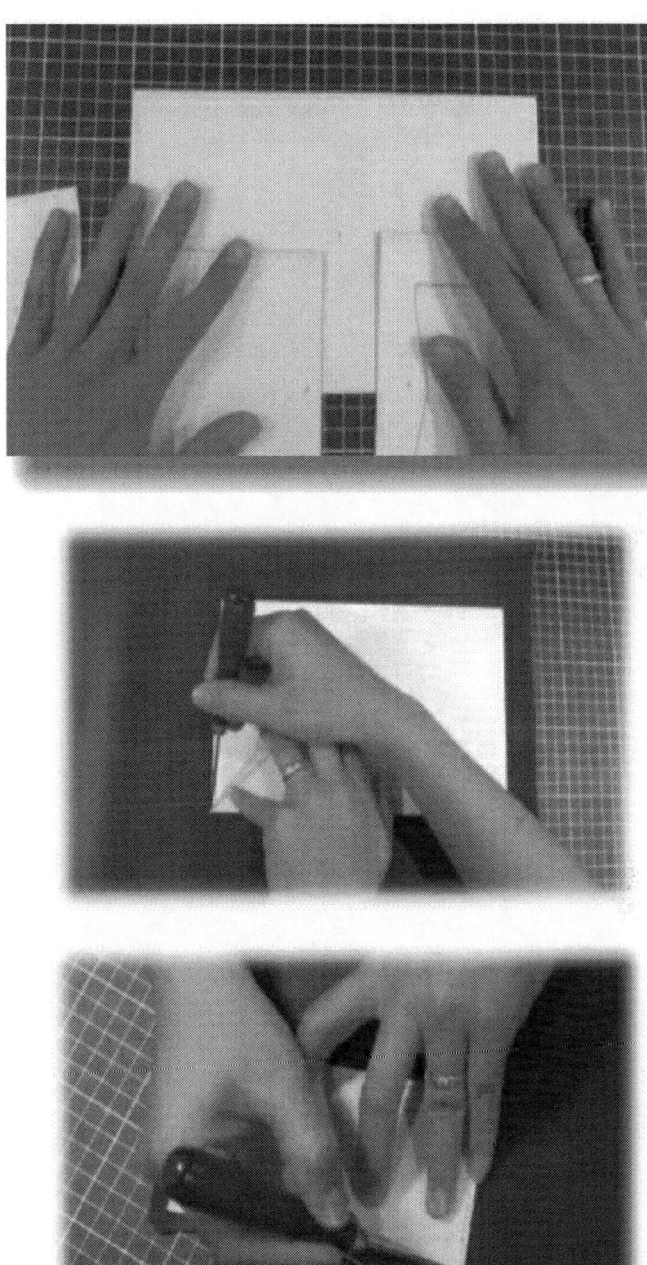

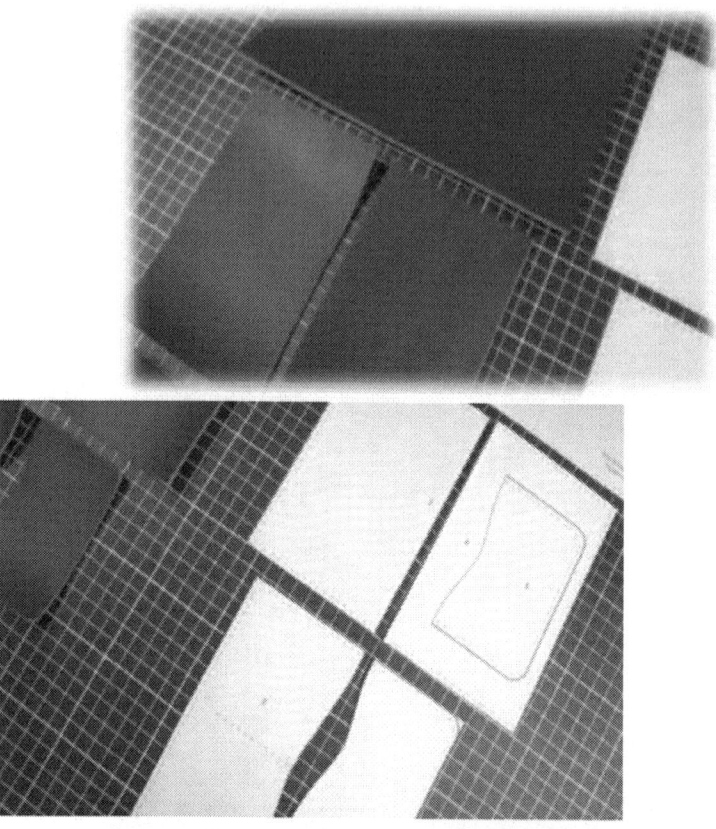

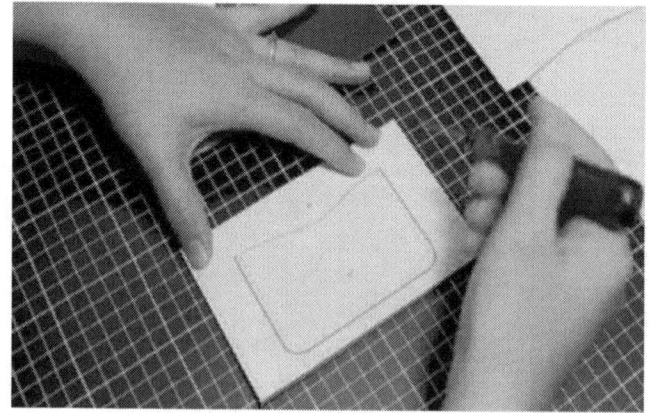

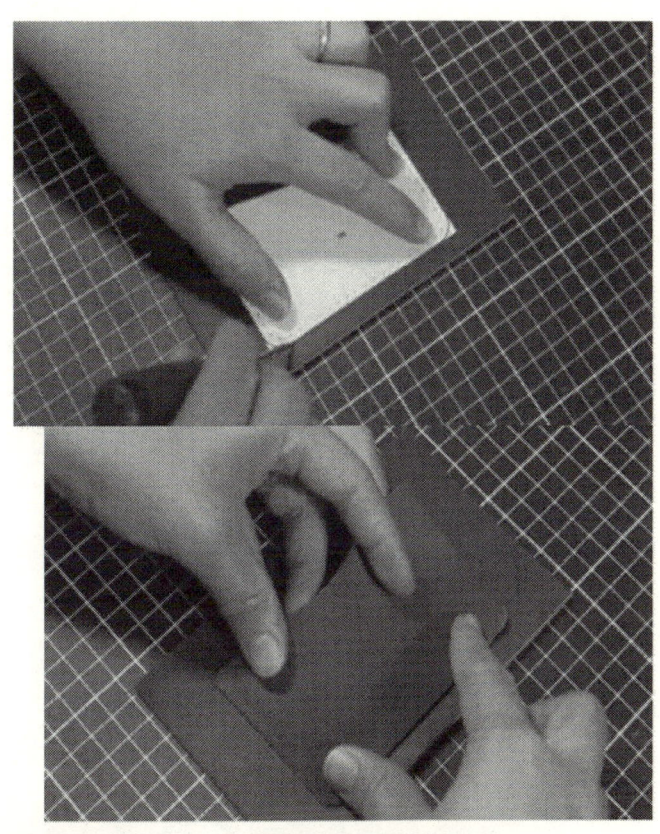

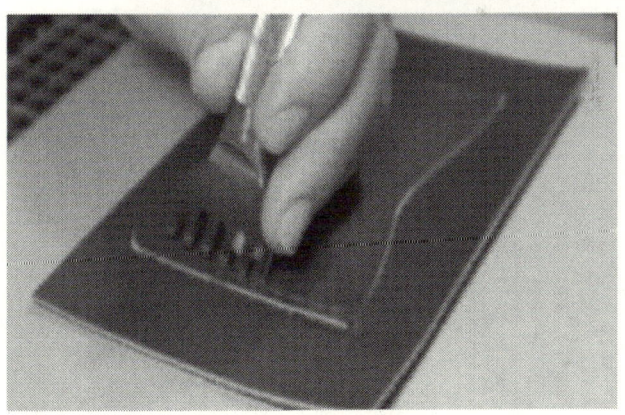

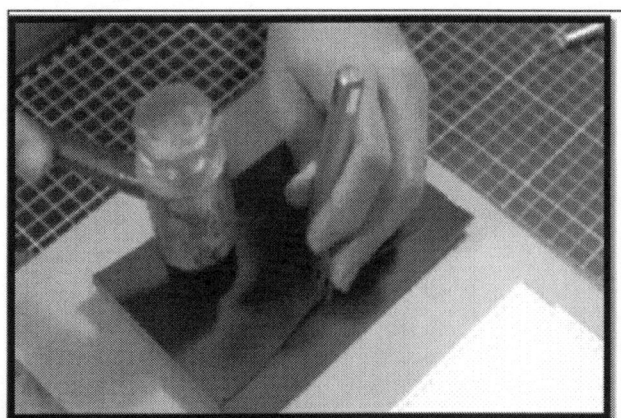

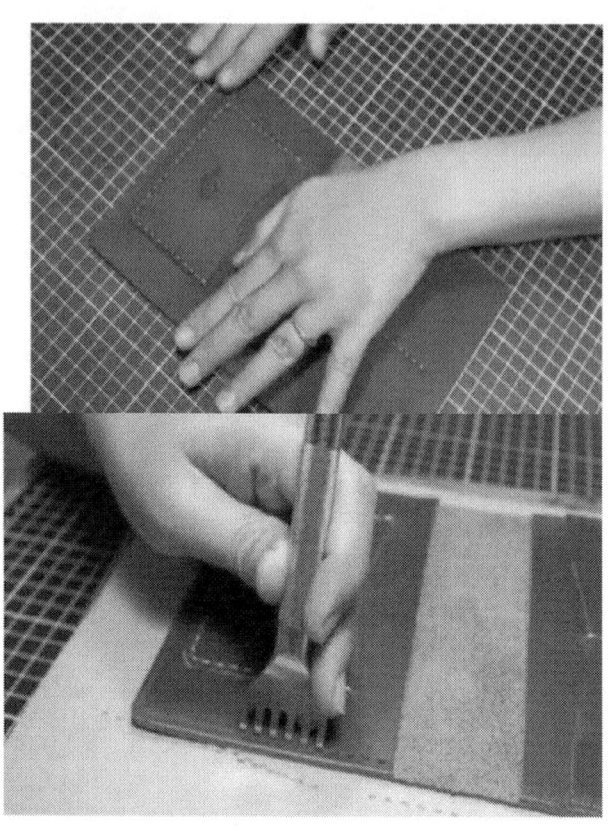

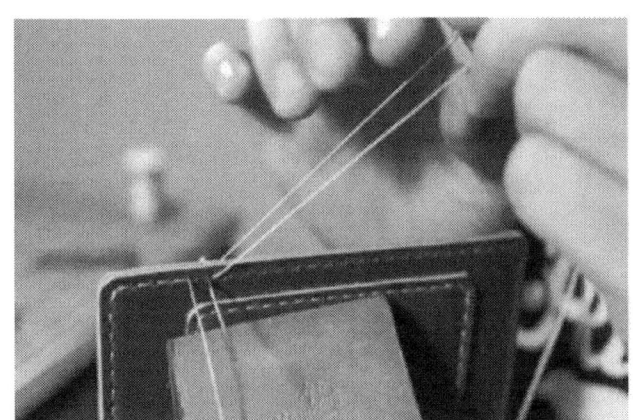

Leather Mason Jar Coozie

Needed materials
Pint-sized Mason jar
Catgut thread
Hammer
Heavy needle
Cutting mat
Knife
Two sets of rivets
Carving leather

Directions
- Cut a piece of leather equivalent to the measurement of your jar, and a thin strand of half to three-quarter inch wide and six inches long.
- Drill six holes on each short side of your jar leather with a leather hole punch or a heavy needle.
- To make the handle, rivet the strip into big leather, with the leather's wrong side on the outside. Turn and rivet the right side at the base. It should form a half heart.
- Punch holes and push the riveting studs through the posterior of the leather. Put the thin strand on it, and place the rivet cap atop it.

- Strike the cap on the stud with a hammer using a firm surface. Twist the strand and push down the second stud. Cap and strike with a hammer to hold it in place. What do you see? An excellent mug handle! You can now carve the leather if you wish.
- You will discover that the handle doesn't wind around the jar completely, not a problem; leather is springy.
- With the heavy needle and catgut, thread the holes on the side firmly so that the corners touch each other.
- Meander it front-to-rear through the holes and fasten it inside the coozie; this will provide a perfect mug shape.
- Fix it round the Mason jar; moisten the leather if it seems challenging to press.

The handle is fantastic, and the rivet looks stunning. Enjoy your drink!

Chapter Nine
Scrap Leather Projects

S mall, shapeless pieces of leather are left after crafting items like a backpack, pouch; it is innovative and beautiful to think of means to transform them into usable items. It is advisable to devise methods of converting junk leather pieces to practical and viable items.

As with fashion, home decoration mirrors individual preference and flair. Leather artistry goes beyond what you can wear, bags, and accessories; it can add an unusual hint of grandeur to an assortment of items. It is crucial to understand the various kinds of leather and the most appropriate type for your project.

Herb Planter Tags

It is well known that a small interior herb garden is attractive by itself, complementing it with a leather herb planter tag can add a touch of grandeur to the plain pot.

Needed materials and instruments
Revolving leather punch hole
Twine or string
Fine-point paint market in silver, white, or gold
x-acto knife
Scrap leather

Directions
-   Cut out rectangular shapes of 1" x 4"
-   Drill holes on any end of the labels.
-   Inscribe the name of your plants on the individual label with the paint pen and dry them.
-   Pass the strings through the hole and tug to fasten the tags on your plant pots, and you there you have it!

Cabinet and Drawer Pulls

Drawer pulls are functional, and they add flair to any second-hand shop dresser renovation project or kitchen cabinet overhaul. This homogenous material style requires minimal effort to create.

Needed materials and instruments:
12" ruler
hammer
x-acto knife
Revolving leather hole punch
Leather scraps
Screwdrivers
Screws

Directions

- Unscrew the original hardware from the cabinet or drawer doors. Estimate the distance between the holes left by the hardware and cut leather strands long enough to overlap on each side and accommodate your hand in the handle after installation.
- Cut designs on the ends or add any hint of style and unique features you love or leave the leather for a simple and more homely look.
- Drill holes in the leather; ensure that the distance is even for the individual strand to guarantee a stable outlook.
- Pass the screws through the holes and fasten the pulls in your cabinet or drawer in appropriate positions.

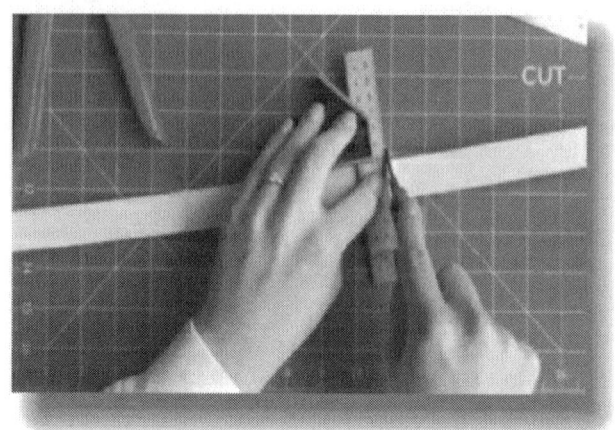

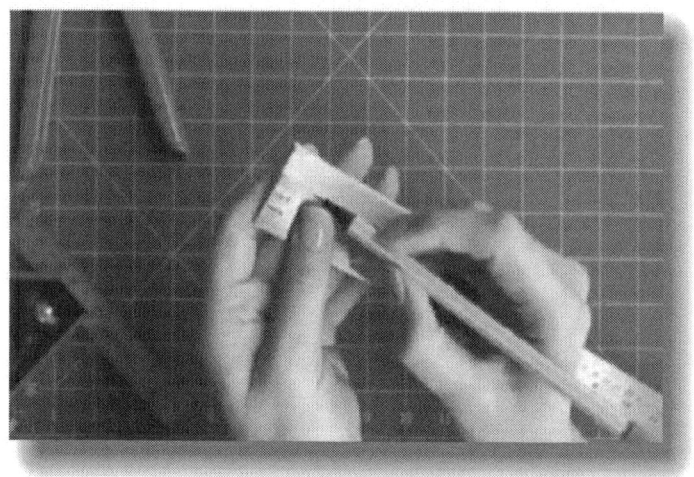

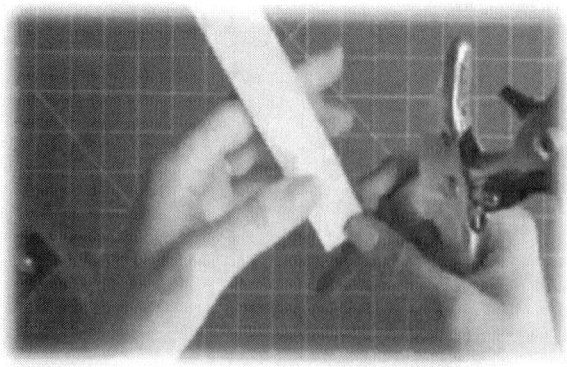

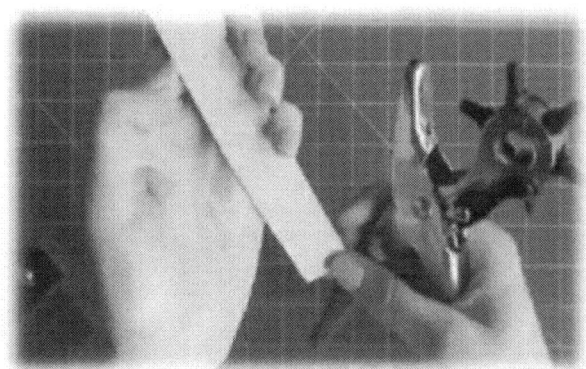

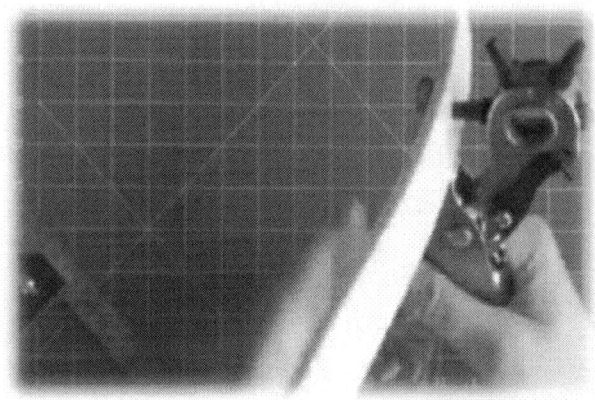

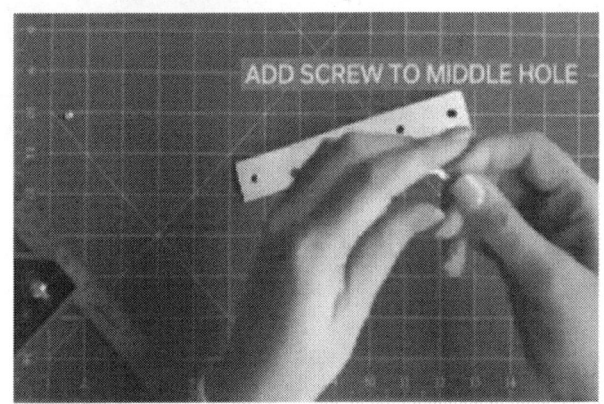

ADD SCREW TO MIDDLE HOLE

Picture frame

Leather can produce a simple, extraordinary, and elegant picture frame. You can get a cheap frame to refurbish is the second-hand store.

Needed materials:
Plain picture frame with even surface
Leather cutting devices
Clamp

Sturdy glue
Leather scraps

Directions

- Measure the exterior corners and breadth of the picture frame. Cut the same length and width of leather strands. Afterward, cut the ends at 45° so that the strands will not intersect when positioned on the frame.
- Attach the strands to the frame with glue and hold with clamp during drying.

Coasters

Leather coasters are simple, at the same time, elegant. You can play around with different colors or create a monochrome set, based on the colors of the scrap leather you have.

Needed Materials and tools
x-acto knife
Paint
English bridle scrap leather
Thread and leather needle

Directions

- Create a stencil in your preferred shape, circles, or squares are recommended. Trace the stencil and cut out the coasters.
- You can choose to leave the coaster plain and pretty or liven with leather stamps, stitching along the corners, or beautifying with a paint tinge.

Tray with leather handles

Decorate your coffee table with a handcrafted tray with leather handles. It is the best place for your appetizers or candles.

Needed materials and tools
Sandpaper
Bronze screws
Wood stain, and a satin cloth or paintbrush
Drill
Sewing machine and thread (by choice)
Scrap lumber

Scrap leather of any type

Directions
- Sand the wood till it's even and flat. Paint the wood with any color of your choice and allow it to dry.
- Cut the scrap leather into strips. Be aware that you want the strips to be plane and even on the board but high enough to lay one's hand.
- This step is not mandatory. Set both strips on each other, with the wrong sides towards each other. Stitch around the corners with a sewing machine. If you want to skip this step, utilize a single-layered fit for a more homely outlook.
- Align the strips with the sides of the board and join using screws.

Napkin rings

Leather napkin rings are easy to make, giving a homey feel to any dinner setup.

Needed Materials and tools
x-acto knife
English bridle scrap leather
Directions

- Cut the junk leather into 0.5" x 6" strands. Wind up a napkin, knot the leather strand around the towel, and exhibit with the knot atop it.

Leather valet tray

For a valet tray, choose a piece of leather that is thick and sturdy enough to maintain its shape. You can either use a dye vegetable bronzed leather (purchase it pre-finished) or choose the kind of leather with the color and feel you desire.

Needed Materials and tools
Copper rivets
Copper burrs
Leather scrap
Marking tools like awl or pencil
Knife
Ball peen hammer or rivet setter
Hole punch
Ruler

Directions
- Settle on the size of the valet. Take several items you intend to place on the tray, lay them out, and measure their trail. Add an inch on every side.
- Mark the valet's exterior shape on leather according to the measurement, including the lines where you will ultimately crimp the leather to form the sides.

Hint: it is preferable to use a metal point for marking because it leaves an imprint that this is simple to trace, and does not require ink, thereby eradicating the problem of ink staining or spillage on the leather. You can use a pen for marking, though.

- Proceed to cut out the leather. There are unique knives for this task like a woodcarver's knife or a head knife, but an essential x-acto knife with a new cutting edge will do it.
- Fold the leather on the engraved line; this boosts the leather's ability to maintain the wanted shapes when the edges are drawn together.
- Hold the four edges in place after drawing them together. Use rivets for this procedure, it appears to be challenging, but it is relatively easy. You can get copper rivet separately at a hardware store in your vicinity, but remember the copper washers that accompany them.
- Find out where to position the rivets. Keep in mind that rivets keep the leather together. If this is your first time using a rivet, get some additional leather scrap and train them before going on with this step.
- Put the rivet in their holes and bang them down firmly. Throw in your wallet and key and you have a fantastic leather beauty before you.

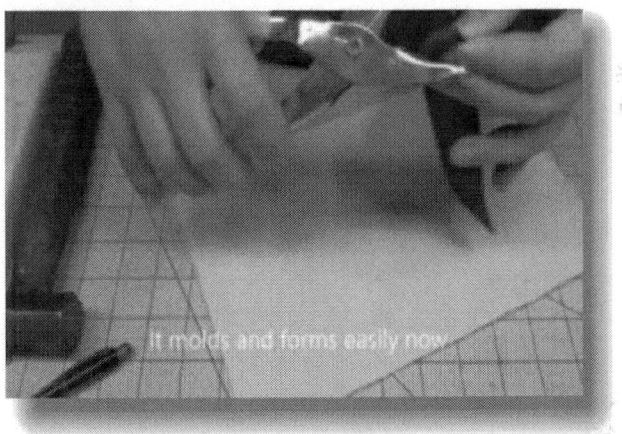

It molds and forms easily now

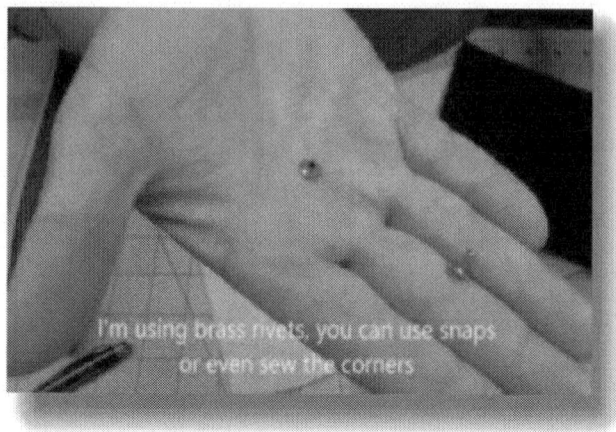

I'm using brass rivets, you can use snaps
or even sew the corners

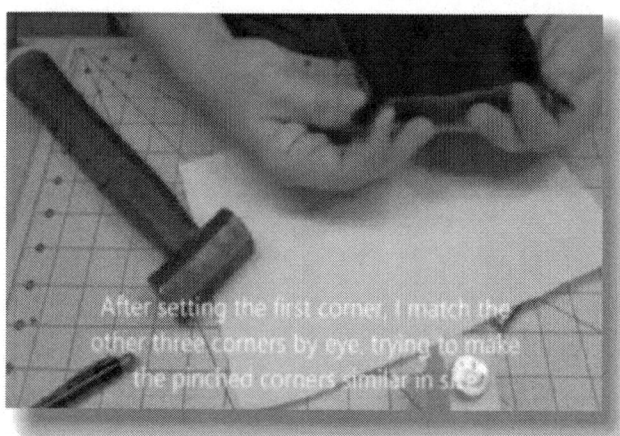

After setting the first corner, I match the
other three corners by eye, trying to make
the pinched corners similar in size

Woven Leather Stool

- Measure the leg height and tick the boards using a square. A perfect square will guarantee an ideal bench. Then, cut the boards. For a rectangular desk, cut out four 18 inch long and 12 inch wide boards.

- Bore your pocket screw guide holes. A cheap pocket guide is available at almost all hardware shops. Fix the pocket guide to the board and bore all your holes.

- Sand the boards to obtain an even outlook. Sanding is more convenient at this stage than after fitting the pieces together. Sanding to a minimum of 220grit will produce a furniture standard surface.

- The next stage is the assembly. Cut a few 3/8 pieces of junk board to aid the placement of the stringers in the middle of the leg pieces before joining. Use some junk to create an even gap between the base stringers and the top. Place a finished side on the work surface before fastening all the screws. Fix both polished ends and proceed to join both with the leftover stringer boards.

-      It is time to apply the finish. I'd suggest Danish oil because the application is convenient, and it produces a fantastic outlook. Obey the guidelines on the can and allow the oil to dry totally before adding straps. A couple of 1 ½ inch strap from a previous project or seatbelt webbing or tapestry strap is the ideal option for the woven top. Cut your belts lengthy enough to wound around your boards. Fix the long pieces before twisting the other ones in one after the other with the help of a tack hammer. It is crucial to space leather straps because they are so thick, to ensure easy weaving. You can weave thin straps tightly.

You are at liberty to explore several different finishes, in different colors.

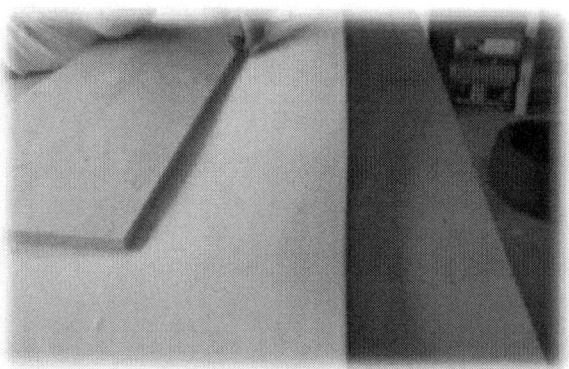

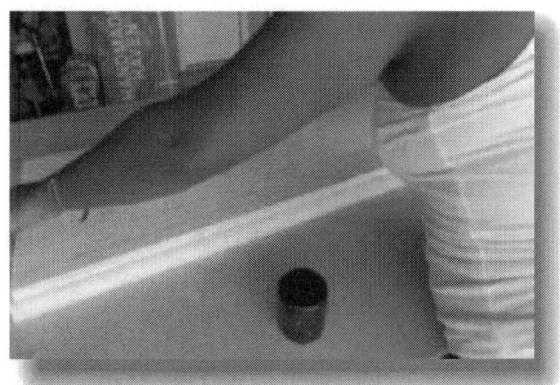

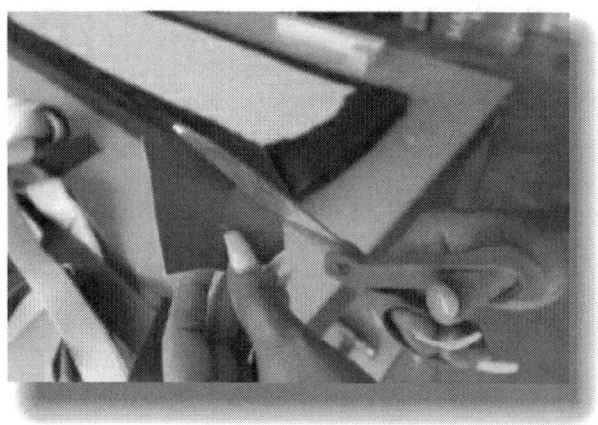

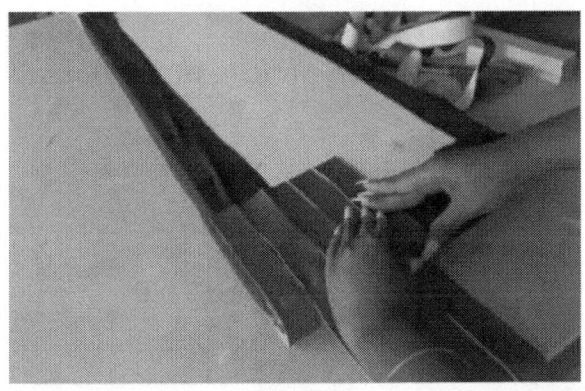

Leather Accent Pillow

Needed materials
Embroidery floss
Poly-fill
Embroidery needle
Cheap but weighty leather

Directions

- Determine the size of the pillow. This procedure will create a small accent pillow of 15 inches squared. Place pieces on a smooth surface, with the outer sides facing each other and the seams in the opposite way. The seams will provide you with a reasonably linear line to trace on every side.
- Sew inside together with a lengthy strip of embroidery floss and embroidery needle; use a simple stitch not longer than half an inch to make sure that the filling won't be visible. You can stitch the three sides in one round if you are confident enough to use a very long strip of embroidery floss. You can use shorter pieces and sew one side at a time. Leave a half to one inch away from the border of the fabric to leave space for crimping; else, the material will crease the between the stitches.
- Secure the stitches with basic overhand knots. After sewing inside completely, go back on the seam to form a sturdier seam. Sturdy seams compel the leather to maintain its shape.
- After sewing the three sides totally, sew the side partially to give space for turning and filling the pillow. Fill the pillow with cheap poly-fill if you are working with a weighty fabric, a pillow form is ideal if you are working with flimsy leather material. Close the space by folding the edges in and sewing a basic but firm stitch between both pieces.

Leather Strap Key Ring

Needed materials
Rotary punch or awl
Rivets and setter
Craft knife
Large-eyed needle
Organic cowhide leather strap
Waxed cotton cord
1 ¼ inch nickel-plated flat keychain
Leather glue
Ribbon
Paint pen

Directions
-   Waxed thread closure: cut a strip of leather according to the desired size.
-   Drill four small holes on the leather strip with awl and mallet. Insert the ring in the strap and twist so that holes line up. Insert the cotton cord in the needle, and sew around the ring to secure it. Stitch around twice and complete with a square knot. Prune the edges with a craft

knife to make it uniform. If you like, complete the sides with paint pens.

- Cut a strand of leather for rivet closure—drill two holes on the sides of the leather strand with a rotary punch or awl and mallet. Insert the ring in the strap and twist so that the holes line up with each other. Set the rivet.

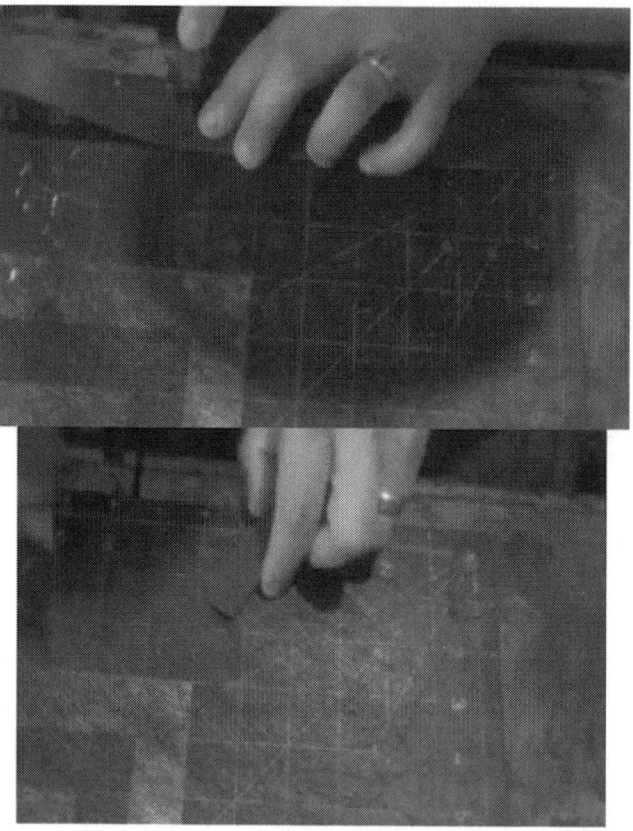

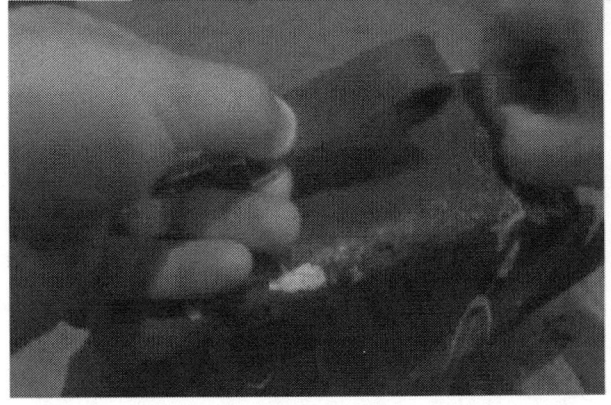

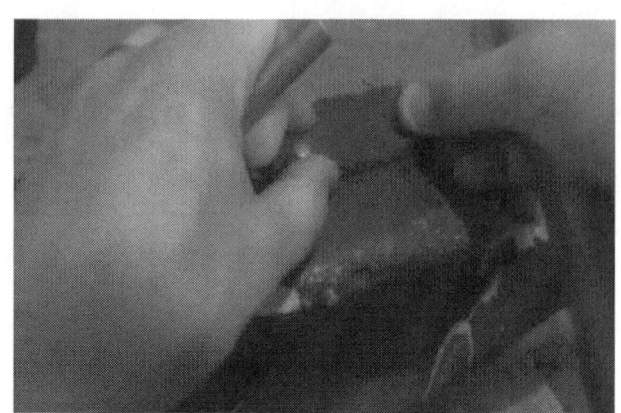

Leather Tablet Case

Materials needed for leather tablet case:

1. Leather
2. Essential leather work instruments

- A rawhide or simple wooden hammer
- A hard surface like granite or marble panel
- Clamps
- Feather design
- Swivel knife
- Some beveling instruments

3. Materials for sewing

- Pliers – for threading
- Leather needles
- Waxed thread or sinew thread
- Creasing tool – to form a fine uniform line on margins before sewing
- Craft-tool stitching groover – dents a passage through the edge for hole drilling and sewing
- Awl – for punching holes in leathers
- Overstitch wheel – marks the position of the holes for uniform stitching

4. Tools for fixing snaps

- Fasteners – in a kit
- A hole punch tool
- Setting tool or setter – for clasping the parts together

5. Materials for leather treatment:

- Leather dye
- Satin sheen
- Leather glue
- Spray bottle containing water

- Disposable gloves, sponge and a piece of cloth

6. Ruler and cutting tools –

Directions
1. Cutting and shaping the leather
Begin by cutting the leather to the desired size, form your tablet or device. If you don't have leather that is lengthy enough, cut two pieces of leather and sew together. Follow the steps below if you are working with two pieces of leather: cut out the leather pieces, use the edge creasing tool on the corners, and moisten the leather to ease folding. Then, go on to give it a simple shape. After drying, cut out the flap piece, use a flimsy material for the flap to effortlessly cut with scissors. Sew the pieces with sinew thread, align the pieces and dampen.

Smear glue on one side of each piece of leather; allow them to sit for a while to get sticky. Put the pieces together and place a weighty object on the attached materials.

After twenty minutes, dampen the leather and use the creasing tool on it. Use the stitching groove afterward to mark sewing lines and then overstitch wheel to produce marks to identify the holes' position. Create slits to stitch through with an awl with the pieces of materials, put a few cutting mats under the leather while doing this. Sew with hand, ensuring that you tug the thread as firmly as you can.

After stitching, you have to reshape the leather. This step is necessary even if you are working with a single piece of leather. Moisten the leather; place your tablet in a plastic wrap or a book that it can fit.

Shape the leather along with the book or plastic wrap and cover it with anything to prevent crinkling marks from nearby items. Place a weighty object on it while it dries. Be cautious with your tablet while doing this, use clamps to hold but be attentive and precise so that you won't mar the leather.

2. Tooling the feather
This step is where it gets interesting. You can carry out any form of tooling you love on your leather piece. Place the stencil on your moistened leather, then use a smoothing tool to flatten and even out the particular stencil you desire to move to the leather. Cut through the lines with a swivel knife.

Moisten the leather again if it gets dry. Use the simple beveling device and mallet starting from the exterior margin of the leather. Strike lightly with the mallet, shift a bit ahead of the line and strike once more, move again and continue and one till you finish the line. Repeat the process with the interior margin; hitting with more pressure will give you a profound contrast and more visible marks.

3. Suede lining for the leather tablet case
Cut out the suede and prime the suede for gluing. Smear the glue uniformly on the leather's interior and a side of the suede with a brush. Let both surfaces dry a bit or till they become sticky, place the suede on the interior of the leather case, and even it out immediately.

You can dye the leather exterior and the interior suede, but if you wish to dye just the leather, it is advisable to do it before setting the suede inside the leather. When the glue is utterly dry, cut off the surplus suede.

4. Adding the interior pieces to hold the tablet
This procedure can be complicated if you are not accurate. You should put the tablet in the middle, and then snap the case shut so you can have an idea of where to set it. Mark the space intended for the tablet with a couple of pins to ascertain the position of holders.

Cut the pieces for the holders; punch a hole on the part that will be on the top left corner if you are working with a kindle instead of the tablet because it has a speaker on the spot where you have the hole. Hold the pieces with glue. Moisten the leather, punch holes in the small pieces with an awl, to sew both longer pieces. Dampen the leather after sewing the pieces together, position them on the tablet the way you'd like them to be, and dry.

After drying, take them off one after the other, and let the base strands intertwine. Punch holes in the appropriate place on the primary piece of leather with the awl. Sew the little pieces of leather to the primary leather piece at three different points to hold them together.

Fix individual corner pieces one after the other, measure and re-measure if the need arises, to ensure that the tablet is positioned correctly.

5. Adding the snap closure
Determine the perfect spot for your closure, as much as you can, ensure that it's in the center, and mark the point. Do the same for the base snap and align it with the upper one. Moisten the leather, punch a hole with the rotary hole punch, and then add the snaps.

Follow the instructions on the snap kit. For the upper snap, there should be a small metal anvil beneath the flat metal piece. The top piece has a cap and socket, while the base piece comprises an eyelet and a stud above it. Afterward, strike the pieces lightly with craft-tool setter and mallet to push them in and hold them in place.

6. Dyeing and finishing the leather

The leather design will look dull without a finish. You can put suede behind the case to shield the stitches. Attach the suede with glue or sew the edges, but it looks more beautiful with gluing. Although it is not ideal to dye suede with leather, it turns out amazing, so try it if you want.

Clean the leather surface with a deglazer, alcohol, or by any other means before dyeing the leather. Try the dye on a junk leather piece before using it on your main leather. You can also try a hi-lighter; this improves the color without totally dyeing it. Use the "dauber" that accompanies the dye to ensure uniform application of stain or a fluffy fabric and allow it to dry completely.

After the dye is dry, apply satin sheen over it. Make sure you wear gloves and use a reasonably moist sponge to rub it in a uniform coat. After it is dry, you can add one or two more layers for a glossy finish.

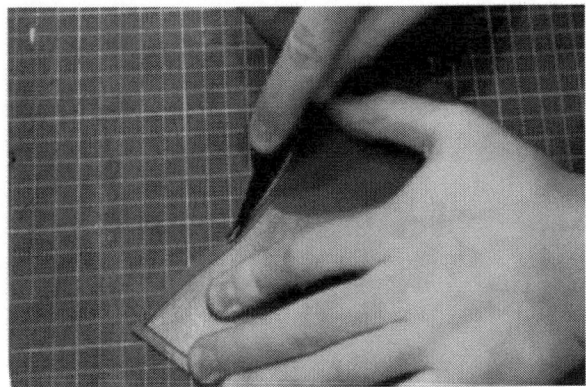

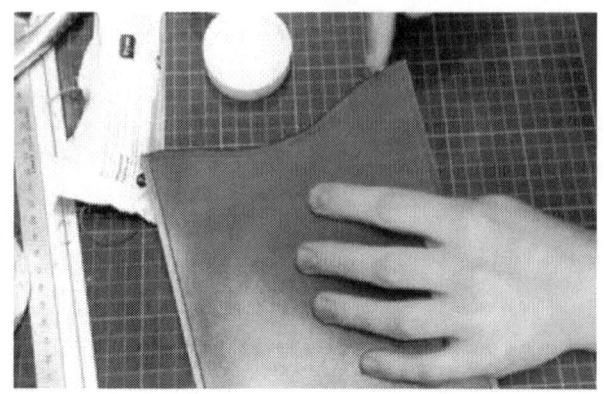

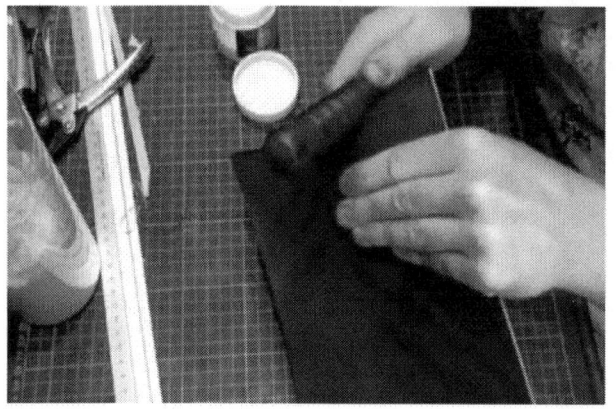

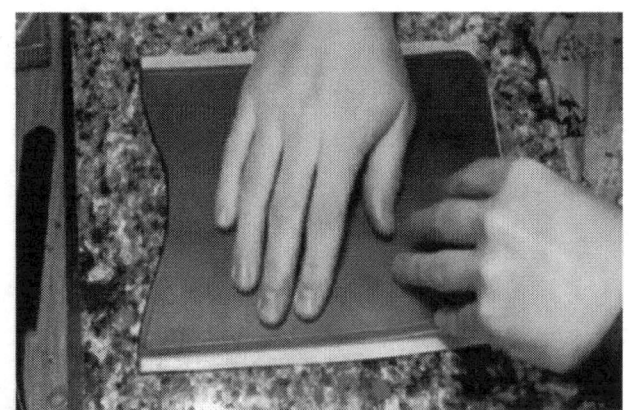

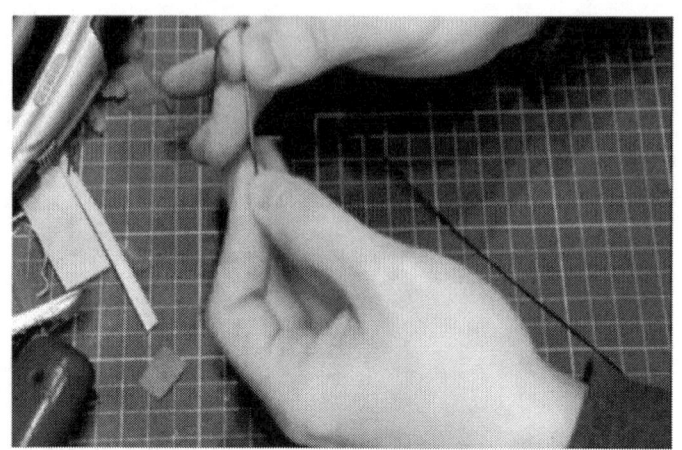

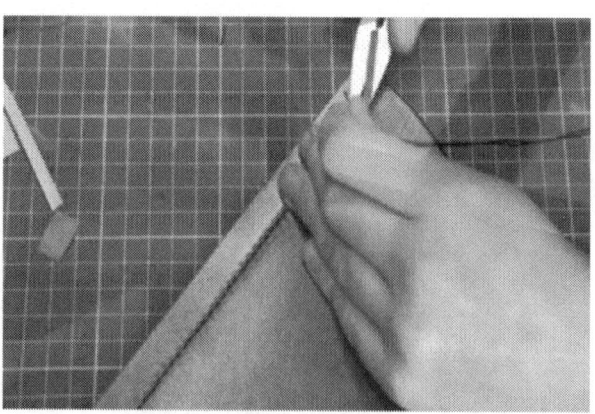

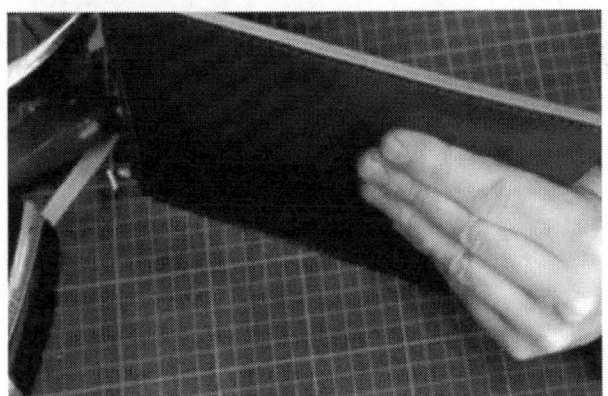

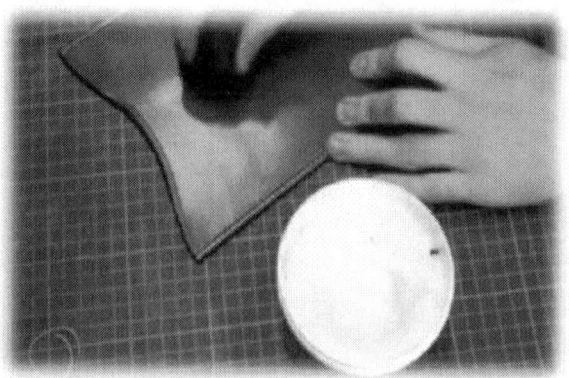

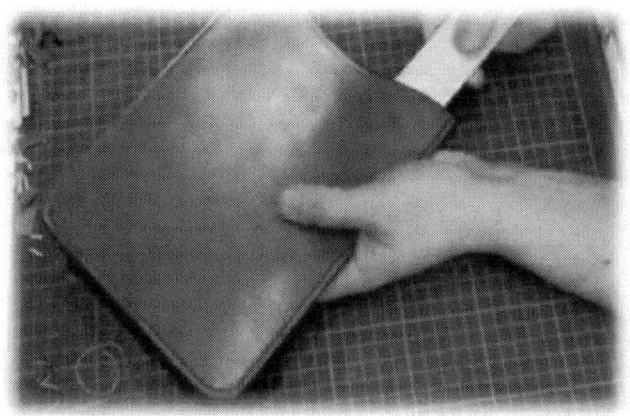

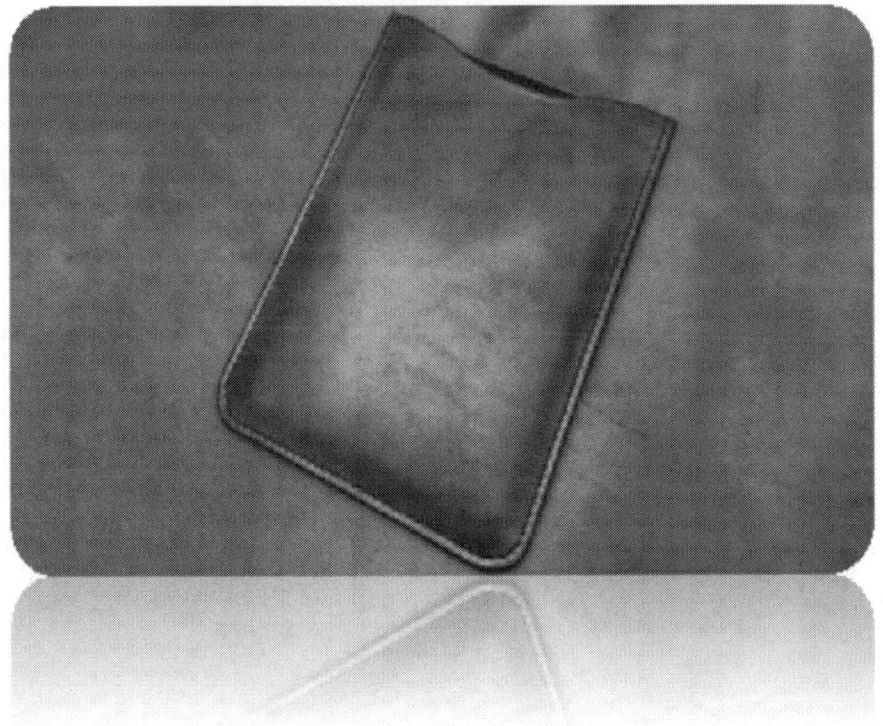

Precautionary Measures

Leatherwork is a worthwhile venture that provides artists with the opportunity to develop expertise, exposure, and experience. Leather kits simplify and ease some projects because the most challenging activity has been accomplished. Designs become trickier as artists build their skills. If you are a learner or an expert, safety is a constant and is very important. Each needful skill in leatherwork is somewhat hazardous if the artist is careless. Below are some essential safety tips for a leather crafter.

Wear protective clothing
The most fundamental thing you can do to protect yourself is to wear clothing that will protect you from unforeseen occurrences. Put on safety goggle, particularly during leather stamping or punching. The steel-toed shoe will protect your leg if heavy equipment should fall. A thick apron will shield your body from wandering material.

Be careful during cutting
Tools with a sharp cutting edge are a necessity in leather artistry. These tools are no respecters of objects, and unfortunately, people too. Ensure that you always cut in the opposite direction of your body, and keep the sharp edges of these tools away from your body.

Keep your fingers away from machinery
Your fingers are your gold; they are essential in crafting but can be obstructive once in a while. Be cautious of machinery during crafting, and always keep your fingers away from the course of the tools. Put a minimum of 1in gap between your fingers and sharp tools. Sewing needles also require a fair dose of your deference.

Ventilate your workshop
You need several chemical solutions to get particular features, some of these chemicals and their fumes are toxic. Ventilate your workspace properly. Wear a respirator to protect yourself from poisonous gas.

Clean your space after every project
Keep tools and materials away after completing a design. It gets the space ready for a subsequent project and puts tools out of harm's way of adults and children. Irrespective of your years of experience, obey the following guidelines to keep yourself and the people around you safe.

Everyone involved in leather artistry must be aware and enlightened about the safe use of every tool.

Check the burner and power cord for signs of damage or malfunction before using them.

Examine all sharp and pounding equipment for extreme battering and deterioration. Check all sharp tools like leather knife, shear blades for bluntness.

Whenever any leather tool or electric burner fails the assessment, notify your parents, guardian, or any other person in charge to take it out.

If any sharp object falls, do not endeavor to grab it.

Use leather shears in consistent, small motions. It is more convenient to use from left to right if you are left-handed and vice-versa.

Don't ever run with sharp objects in hand. Hold them with great care and a minimum of one inch away from the sharp edges.

Strike the mallet or hammer with the head down with consistent pressure. Do not over-exert the pressure during striking.

When a hot electric burner is not in use, put it in tool rest. Unplug the burner from power /source when you are no longer using it.

Don't ever use fractured or damaged needles or awls to sew.

Wear gloves during the application of leather stains. After applying stain on sponge or cloth, cover the container before applying it to the leather.

If you get hurt during crafting, inform the authority figure if the wound is not severe, clean with soap and water, and put a neat bandage on it. Seek immediate medical care if the injury is severe.

Made in the USA
Columbia, SC
27 November 2023